"Beth Brickell has gone where no one else has been before. She has written a compelling account of the Brickells, early Miami's most important family."
—DR. PAUL S. GEORGE, professor of history, Miami-Dade College; historian to the Historical Association of Southern Florida

"Beth Brickell has created an important work. She has succeeded in putting a human face on two of the icons of Miami history, William and Mary Brickell. She goes on to make an excellent case for declaring Mary Brickell the true 'Mother of Miami.' It is extremely well researched, organized, documented and written."
—TIM ROBINSON, author, *A Tropical Frontier: Pioneers and Settlers of Southeast Florida*

"Beth Brickell's new book on the history of the Brickell family in Miami is both groundbreaking and explosive, for in this book Ms. Brickell puts to rest a number of 'Miami myths.' Her superb book is the work of one who was obsessed not only with facts but with truth. She has done an outstanding, if not incredible, job with her completely researched, exhaustively documented and factual tome."
—SETH H. BRAMSON, adjunct professor of history, Barry University, Miami Shores and Florida International University, Miami

"Thanks to Beth Brickell's diligent work, the whole story of the 'founding parents' of Miami and Fort Lauderdale can finally be told."
—PATRICK SCOTT, attorney/historian, Fort Lauderdale

"Beth Brickell has written a fascinating account of the life of two south Florida pioneers too often overlooked, Mary and William Brickell. This wife and husband team forged a new life in the heat and storms of the old hunting grounds of the Tequesta and Seminoles. Whether taking on William Gleason, Henry Flagler or rival real estate developers, they never flinched and helped to create modern Miami."
—DR. JOE KNETSCH, state historian, Tallahassee

William and Mary BRICKELL

Founders of Miami & Fort Lauderdale

Beth Brickell

Charleston · London

THE
History
PRESS

Published by The History Press
Charleston, SC 29403
www.historypress.net

Front cover, top left: tintype of William Brickell, *courtesy of Historical Museum of Southern Florida*; *top right*: tintype of Mary Brickell, *Carmen Petsoules Collection*; *bottom*: Brickell Point, 2009, *photo by Beth Brickell*.
Back cover: *Carmen Petsoules Collection*.

First published 2011

Manufactured in the United States

ISBN 978.1.60949.213.7

Library of Congress Cataloging-in-Publication Data
Brickell, Beth.
William and Mary Brickell : founders of Miami and Fort Lauderdale / Beth Brickell.
p. cm.
Includes bibliographical references.
ISBN 978-1-60949-213-7
1. Brickell, William B., d. 1908. 2. Brickell, Mary, d. 1922. 3. Miami (Fla.)--History--19th
century. 4. Miami (Fla.)--Biography. 5. Miami (Fla.)--History--20th century. I. Title.
F319.M6B76 2010
975.9'381--dc22
2010049064

For my dad and Carmen

Contents

Acknowledgements

I AM DEEPLY GRATEFUL TO TWO PEOPLE in particular, without whom this book would not have been possible. Carmen Petsoules, a passionate advocate of William and Mary Brickell, made available to me her forty-year collection of Brickell documents and photographs that she had never shared with another historian, some of which she received directly or indirectly from members of the Brickell family. Her work gave me an important foundation to begin my own research. Moreover, her advice was invaluable. Since I am not a resident of South Florida and was unfamiliar with what had been written by others, research would have been very difficult without her guidance—pointing me to relevant sources of information and making me aware of books and newspaper articles that I needed to absorb.

Other essential support came from Patrick Scott, an attorney and historian in Fort Lauderdale. I was so impressed with the conscientious and detailed research he had done for his article in the *Broward Legacy*, "The Many Heirs of Jonathan Lewis," that I called and introduced myself. Pat immediately offered to help with advice and guidance. He also gave me documents that are not readily available in libraries and museums and read every draft of my work, pointing out mistakes and suggesting additional sources and areas that I should cover in my research and writing.

Also helping me with valuable notes and suggestions upon reading the manuscript were distinguished Florida historians Dr. Paul George, Dr. Joe Knetsch and Professor Seth H. Bramson.

An important resource for research was Denise McMahon, an Australian who, with her partner, Christine Wild, has uncovered extensive details about the activities of William Brickell and his partner, Adam Kidd, during the Australian gold rush of the 1850s. After reading what they had discovered about William in their book, *American Fever, Australian Gold*, and an article they wrote for *Tequesta*, "William Barnwell Brickell in Australia," I e-mailed Denise with many questions that she very graciously answered. She also shared documents with me and pointed to online sources that allowed me to find new information about William that I may not have found otherwise.

Many librarians, historians and genealogists, too numerous to name, did research for me in Ohio, Pennsylvania, California, Washington, D.C., Australia and Florida, and I'm very grateful for their help. Especially important was daily help given to me for many weeks by Robin Betancourt, court records specialist at the Miami-Dade County Recorder's Office/Records Library, when I was meticulously searching for deeds, plats and legal documents. John Shipley, manager of the Helen Muir Florida Collection at the Miami-Dade Public Library, gave me access to materials in the library vault that I wouldn't have known about without his help. Also, the staff of the Archives and Research Center at the Historical Museum of Southern Florida was beneficial to my research.

Lastly, I want to acknowledge and thank those who have given permission to reprint photographs: Carmen Petsoules for photos of a young Mary, a portrait painting of William, a tintype of Mary, an elderly Mary with daughter Maude, a widow, Manuel Carbonell's bas-relief for the Brickell bridge, The Roads commemoration plaque, several photos of nineteenth-century Brickell Point, Carmen and Butch Brickell, Carmen holding up the "Mother and myself" photo, The Roads 1923 auction site and Rosabelle Peacock; the Historical Museum of Southern Florida in Miami for photos of Julia Tuttle, Alice Brickell, Maude Brickell, the Royal Palm Hotel postcard, the first Brickell house, the later Brickell mansion, the first train to Miami postcard, the Seminoles postcard, the nineteenth-century sailboat, the road through Brickell Hammock, Brickell Point with marl on the bank and tintype of William; the James Edmundson Ingraham Papers, Department of Special and Area Studies Collections, George A. Smathers Libraries, University of Florida in Gainesville for the James E. Ingraham headshot; Ohio Historical Society for the illustration of the 1797 Steubenville, Ohio town square; Albury, Australia City Collection for illustration of the Exchange Hotel; *TV Guide Magazine*, LLC © 1968 for the *TV Guide Magazine* cover; the National Frontier Trails Museum, Independence, Missouri, for the photo of the 1850 Independence, Missouri town square; the San Francisco History Center, San Francisco Public Library for photos of the 1849 San Francisco harbor and 1849 hotel; Flagler Museum Archives for the 1909 headshot of Henry Flagler; Western Reserve Historical Society, Cleveland, Ohio, for the photo of John D. Rockefeller and Lucy Spelman; and photographer Thomas Nagy for the re-creation of circled wagons. I took the 2009 Miami photos of Brickell Point, Brickell Park and Brickell Avenue and designated the lots given to Flagler by the Brickells and Tuttle on the Miami and Fort Lauderdale plats. All other photos and illustrations are in the public domain or public record.

Beth Brickell
Beverly Hills, California
January 2011

Introduction

Inaccuracies about
the Brickells

I T WAS MY DAD, CARTER RALEIGH BRICKELL, who interested me in the
Miami and Fort Lauderdale Brickells. I had known vaguely of William
and Mary Brickell because I had been in Miami on and off between 1967
and 1969 starring in a CBS television series, *Gentle Ben*, with Dennis Weaver,
Clint Howard and a 650-pound bear. We filmed interiors at the old Ivan Tors
Studios in North Miami on NE 16th Avenue, now Greenwich Studios, and
exteriors in the Everglades.

During the two years I was in the city I learned there was a Brickell Avenue,
and someone took me to see it. At that time, houses and small apartment
buildings lined the boulevard. I was told that it was named after pioneers
William and Mary Brickell, but I didn't learn anything more about the Brickells
except that Miamians pronounced our common name with an emphasis on
the first syllable instead of the last, the way our family pronounced it.

Then, in 1985, my dad retired and took up genealogy as a hobby. He became
interested in William and Mary Brickell, although they are not related to our
family as far as we know. He contacted Dr. Thelma Peters, former president
of the Florida Historical Society and author of three books on early Dade
County: *Biscayne Country 1870–1926*, *Lemon City* and *Miami 1909*. Until
her death in 1996, Dr. Peters and my dad exchanged letters, and she sent him
whatever scant information was available about the Brickells in newspaper
articles. She explained, "Up to this point no historian has undertaken to
write a story of the Brickells. Perhaps this is because the family is regarded as
reclusive and it is hard to do a biography without family cooperation."[1] Maybe
my dad then told Dr. Peters of an eighteen-article investigative series about an

Dennis Weaver, Beth Brickell, Clint Howard and Ben.

unsolved disappearance case in my hometown of Camden, Arkansas, that I had recently investigated and written for the state newspaper, the *Arkansas Gazette.* In a follow-up letter, she wrote, "Indeed it would be great if sometime in the future she would turn her talent to doing a book on the Brickell family."[2] Although I don't remember my dad passing the idea on to me, perhaps he did and it seeped into my unconscious.

Dr. Peters also told my dad about Carmen Petsoules, a Cuban American activist and amateur historian in Miami who had a passionate interest in William and Mary Brickell. He then corresponded with Carmen for eleven years until he passed away in 2002. Both he and Carmen believed that William and Mary had not been given proper recognition for their contribution to Miami and Fort Lauderdale, and he encouraged Carmen to do what she could to make Floridians more aware of the importance of the Brickells to the history of South Florida.

In 1978, I graduated from the American Film Institute in Los Angeles with an MFA in film and became a writer-director. I had intended to make a movie in the spring of 2009 in Arkansas, but I couldn't get the financing because of the economic recession. So, having some downtime, I decided to go to Miami for the first time in forty years to see how it had changed.

Wow! How it had changed! I was so impressed with the gleaming white and glass high-rises in every direction, especially along Brickell Avenue, which had become the financial center of Miami and of commerce throughout the Americas. Not only did the boulevard have the largest concentration of international banks in the United States, but it was now the glamorous address in Miami for high-rise condominium and apartment towers. Moreover, any business within several blocks coveted the Brickell name. Mary Brickell Village, a two-block open mall on Miami Avenue between SW 9th and 11th

Streets, was the go-to social hub for restaurants and businesses south of the Miami River. Brickell Key, east of the northeastern side of Brickell Avenue, was a gated island of upscale, high-rise residential and hotel towers.

I had planned to stay two days in Miami on my way to and from a week in Key West to work on a screenplay, but one look at the city and my plans changed. I couldn't think of a reason in the world to hurry back to the winter cold and wet of Arkansas when I could bask in the sunshine and explore fabulous Miami.

My first phone call was to Carmen. Upon mentioning my father, she immediately invited me to her home in The Roads, a Mary Brickell subdivision. It's impossible to be with Carmen for five minutes and not be affected by her passionate admiration of William and Mary Brickell. And as soon as she learned that I had a BA with a major in history from the University of Arkansas and a background as a newspaper reporter mixed in with my film experience, she determined that I was the person to pull together and do something with her forty years of research on the Brickells. It's hard to say no to Carmen Petsoules!

I was to spend the next many months studying Carmen's collection and searching for additional information about William and Mary in museums, libraries, universities and other sources in Florida, California, Ohio, Pennsylvania, Washington, D.C. and Australia.

MY RESEARCH LED TO AN EARLY CONCLUSION about a photo enlarged to poster size on Carmen's living room wall that had been widely used as a portrayal of Mary Brickell. I didn't believe it was Mary. At first it was just a hunch that a young woman whom a handsome, wealthy William would marry in Australia and bring to the United States would be prettier. And it seemed to me that the Mary who became a Realtor, shrewdly ran the family

Widow photograph.

business of platting and selling their vast stretches of land, played a big role in getting Henry Flagler to bring a railroad to Miami and left her heirs between $5 and $6 million ($64 to $76 million in 2008)[3] wouldn't have looked as old-fashioned as the woman in the photo.

Carmen shared with me the history of the photograph. It was given to her by Carol Snyder of Ocala, Florida, who was the granddaughter of Mrs. DeMarise Purdy, companion and housekeeper of Maude Brickell, youngest daughter of William and Mary and the last to live in the family home at 501 Brickell Avenue. Snyder told Carmen that her grandmother said the picture was of Mary.

Subsequently, Stan Cooper, an amateur historian who passed away in 1998, pointed out to Carmen an interesting detail in the photo. He told her that the woman was a widow because she's wearing a black band beneath her wedding ring. According to Cooper, this was a nineteenth-century tradition signifying the status of a widow.

The black band authenticated my hunch! Mary Brickell wasn't a widow until she was seventy-two years old. The woman in the photo is much younger, in her thirties or forties. At first Carmen dismissed my belief about the widow's age, pointing to a streak of gray that she appears to have in her hair. But, I argued, some women develop gray in their hair at a young age. Moreover, the highlight could be a flare from the photographer's lights. And I added a personal opinion that women in their seventies aren't likely to have a formal photograph made of themselves.

The one photograph that is definitely of Mary Brickell is a snapshot taken with her daughter Maude that appears to have been made close to her death in 1922 at age eighty-

Mary Brickell and daughter Maude.

six. Maude is wearing a dress and hat of a style that was fashionable in the 1920s. Carmen discovered the photograph in 1992 among a collection at the Historical Museum of Southern Florida in Miami. She recognized Maude from her hat, which was the same hat Maude had worn in other known photos, but Carmen wondered who the elderly lady was in the picture with her. She turned over the snapshot and discovered a handwritten inscription: "Mother and myself." Very excited, Carmen realized that she had found the first known photograph of Mary Brickell!

Carmen shared a copy of the photo with me and suggested that we enlarge the older Mary's face to study it better. I did so and placed the enlargement side by side with an enlargement of the widow. I then asked Carmen, "Do you think anyone could age and change facial features this much in ten years between her seventies and her eighties?" "No," she said.

Carmen was understandably chagrined. Because of her conviction that the widow in the photo was Mary, it had become the standard photograph of Mary Brickell for local historians and journalists. It had even been used as Mary's likeness by a sculptor who fashioned a bust for a monument commemorating Mary on Brickell Avenue and by another artist who created a bas-relief depicting Mary for the Brickell Avenue bridge.

Enlargements from photograph of widow and snapshot of Mary Brickell.

The mistaken identity occurred because of a hazy childhood memory. Snyder recalled playing at the Brickell estate when she was a child and told Carmen that her grandmother said the photograph was of Mary. But Snyder was only thirteen years old when her grandmother died in 1961, and she was recalling the identification decades later.

Carmen spoke of another mistake Snyder made. Snyder offered to sell a ring to Carmen that she said had belonged to Mary and was the same ring the widow was wearing in the photograph. But the ring Snyder sent to Carmen had a black stone, while the widow's ring in the photograph has a white stone that appears to be a pearl.

THE WIDOW IS LIKELY MARY'S MOTHER, Catherine Merriman Bulmer, born June 17, 1811, in Castle Donington, Leicestershire, England.[4] Catherine was only forty-six years old when her husband, Joseph, died on May 23, 1858. The dress the widow is wearing is typical of women's fashions in the 1850s to early 1860s. Perhaps Mary wanted a photograph of her mother to take with her to the United States when she and William left Australia in 1862. If the photo, a tintype, was taken not long after Joseph's death in 1858, that would explain why Catherine is wearing a black band beneath her ring.

Catherine and Joseph Bulmer were not sophisticated. When they married in Manchester, England, on December 25, 1832, neither could read nor write, and they signed their names on the register with an x.[5]

Mary Bulmer Brickell.

A TINTYPE GIVEN TO THE Historical Museum of Southern Florida by Stan Cooper is more likely a true photo of Mary. He rescued it from debris at the Brickell mansion before it was torn down in 1961. Markings on the back of the tintype state that it was professionally made in Worcester, Massachusetts.[6] Although William and Mary never lived in Massachusetts, they traveled a great deal in the 1860s when they lived in Pennsylvania and Ohio prior to the family moving to South Florida in 1871. According to a historical sketch written by Maude about her parents, the family also lived in Washington, D.C., during this period.[7] Mary was in her late twenties and early thirties in the 1860s, and the woman in the photograph appears to be in that age range.

A matching tintype of William also was rescued and given to the museum by Cooper. It was made in Brooklyn, New York. We know for certain that William was in Brooklyn because he bought a yacht there in 1873, which he named the *Ada* after his mother, Adelaide Stanhope Brickell.

William Barnwell Brickell.

The facial features of the woman in Cooper's tintype are the same as those of a woman in three other photographs taken at various stages of life that were given to the museum by Snyder.

Howard Kleinberg, former editor of the *Miami News*, contacted Snyder in 1992 about the photos. She told him they had been in a tin box filled with Brickell family photographs that came into her possession after her grandmother died.[8]

According to a newspaper article by Kleinberg, markings on the backs of the three photographs from Snyder follow the history of where Mary lived. The youngest, a tintype, was taken professionally in Melbourne, Australia. Mary lived in Australia from age three to twenty-five. A second was taken in Cleveland, where she lived in her early thirties. The third is the previously mentioned snapshot taken with Maude in Miami when Mary was well into her eighties.[9]

As I continued my research, I was to find other inaccuracies of how Mary and William Brickell have been represented to history. Following is a carefully documented chronology of this fascinating couple that I believe, based on my findings, contributed more to the founding of Miami and Fort Lauderdale than any other South Florida pioneer.

Chapter 1

The Pioneer Spirit of William Brickell

S OME HAVE WONDERED WHY A WEALTHY William Brickell would bring a wife and children to settle in a rough wilderness south of the Miami River in 1871, decades before a city was established. At the time only Seminole Indians and the families of twelve squatters lived between what is now Palm Beach and Key Largo. Perhaps the answer lies in the fact that striking out as a pioneer was in William's heritage.

William's ancestor, a staunch Presbyterian, left Scotland for Ireland because of religious persecution.[10] Then in the mid-1700s, William's great-grandfather was one of four Scotch-Irish brothers who emigrated from Ireland to Fort Redstone, Pennsylvania, near Pittsburgh, when the area was a dense forest inhabited by Indians. His great-grandfather continued west across the Ohio River and settled in what would become Steubenville, Ohio, an unofficial suburb of Pittsburgh.[11]

In 1791, William's relative John Brickell was captured by Delaware Indians near Pittsburgh when he was ten years old and lived with them for four years before being released. Afterward, he continued to live as a Native American in what would become Columbus, Ohio. John Brickell is considered by many to be the first white settler of that city.[12]

STEUBENVILLE, OHIO, WAS PLATTED AS A TOWN in 1797, and William was born there on May 22, 1825. He was named after his father, William Barnwell Brickell. His mother was Adelaide Stanhope Brickell. In the family were three sons, George, Peter and William, and three daughters, Elizabeth, Mary and Sarah.[13]

William Sr. passed away on April 16, 1843, when William Jr. was seventeen years old.[14] His mother had died earlier. At the time of his death, William's

Illustration of Steubenville, Ohio, 1797.

father, a wholesale spirit merchant, owned the property on which the family home was located and had assets from an 1841 sale of several other city lots.[15] His will granted $5 ($114 in 2008) to each of his sons, all of whom had reached maturity, and provided for the guardianship of the three daughters, all younger than fifteen years old. The will also granted the daughters an equal share of any remaining assets upon reaching maturity.[16]

As a young man on his own, William at first engaged in farming and followed mercantile pursuits in Steubenville,[17] a town of seven thousand people at the time.[18] Then, in 1849, his pioneer spirit was aroused with the sensational news from California that gold had been discovered at Sutter's Mill on the American River near San Francisco. He was twenty-four years old. With both parents gone and nothing holding him in Steubenville, William was ready to strike out on his first adventure.

"Gold! Gold! On the American River!" shouted in the streets of San Francisco electrified the nation and the world. Fortune seekers flooded the new city of San Francisco, gateway to the gold fields.

In 1849, an estimated forty-two thousand "Forty-Niners" came to San Francisco by land and another thirty-nine thousand by sea.[19] They traveled overland in ox-drawn wagons across the treacherous plains and deserts of the West and the formidable Rocky Mountains. Others journeyed by steamer to the Isthmus of Panama and crossed a fever-ridden jungle on foot before continuing by ship to San Francisco. Still others sailed from the East Coast sixteen thousand miles around Cape Horn at the southern tip of South America.

John Sutter's sawmill located in Coloma, California, on the bank of the American River.

The young men of Steubenville were as excited about the prospect of finding gold in California as everyone else. A company calling itself the California Mining Company was organized during the winter of 1848–49 consisting of fifty-nine members from Steubenville and the vicinity. William Brickell was one of its members.[20]

A journal kept by one of the young men in the group, Samuel R. Dundass, recorded their momentous experience. He wrote that on Sunday evening before leaving Steubenville the group "marched in a body to one of the churches of the city," where they were addressed "in the most solemn and appropriate language" by two clergymen of the Methodist Episcopal Church. The next day they received another "eloquent oration" by a city luminary while "numbers of citizens flocked to the wharf to bid farewell to friends."[21]

On March 24, 1849, the company left Steubenville on the steamboat *Germantown* headed for St. Louis. There they transferred to the steamer *Mary Blane*, which took them west to Independence, Missouri, the jumping-off place for the Oregon-California Trail. According to Dundass, they arrived at Independence on April 7, pitched camp near the landing in drenching rain and spent the next two weeks purchasing oxen, wagons and provisions for the overland journey.

A citizen from a nearby town described the scene that William and the others experienced:

> *Being at leisure one day, I rode over to Independence. The town was crowded. A multitude of shops had sprung up to furnish*

Illustration of Independence, Missouri town square in 1850.

emigrants and the traders with necessities for their journey; and there was an incessant hammering and banging from a dozen blacksmiths' sheds where the heavy wagons were being repaired and the horses and oxen shod. The streets were thronged with men, horses and mules.[22]

On April 24, the men of the Steubenville company drove their wagons out of Independence. Dundass wrote, "We made quite an imposing appearance with twenty large, covered, six-ox wagons, and sixty men armed and equipped according to western style."[23]

No time was lost in getting a taste of the hardships awaiting them. Dundass recorded:

May 3. Were up and on march at an early hour, but a cold and incessant rain rendered it uncomfortable for the men and slippery and laborious for the oxen. We came to the Chaw Wow River in the forenoon, in the crossing of which we were detained several hours... Being considerably swollen from recent rain, it was now very high and scarcely fordable at all. The banks were steep and abounding in

Re-creation of a wagon train.

the deepest mud and the road extremely narrow. We were compelled to let our wagons down by a long cable and double our teams in ascending the opposite bank.[24]

After two weeks on the trail, the company decided to make a change:

May 8. Our company had organized for the purpose of emigrating together and milling in California as a joint stock company, but having become impressed with the conviction that small trains could travel much faster than large ones...a meeting of the company was called and a resolution adopted to dissolve into companies of tens. We crossed the Kansas together on the 9th and encamped three miles from the river where we remained until the 12th, dividing our teams, wagons and provisions.[25]

William was not in Dundass's smaller group, but his experience was similar in crossing the continent as the two groups of ten wagons followed each another. They traveled on average between eight and twenty-two miles a day, and the hardships they endured are unimaginable today. The one nice surprise was that the Indians along the trail were friendly and occasionally interacted with the travelers for trade or simple curiosity. Everything else drove the men to a breaking point.

They had to constantly ford rivers and streams and help push wagons up steep banks of mud. They walked and slept in torrential rains, hail and hurricane-force winds. They often ran out of drinking water and suffered thirst. They walked for days on end under a blistering hot sun on miles of trail that was foot-deep in sand or choking dust.

One man in Dundass's group was separated from his horse and drowned when attempting to cross a swift river. A ten-year-old boy in William's group accidentally shot and killed himself while unloading provisions from a wagon. Oxen gave out and dropped dead. Wagonloads had to be constantly lightened by throwing out provisions, even foodstuffs. Wagons broke down and were left behind. One excitement came with a herd of buffalo that allowed the men to replenish their meager food supplies.

The men finally straggled into San Francisco on November 12, seven and a half months after leaving Steubenville.[26] William Brickell was one of the members of the Steubenville company who made it there.

But it wasn't to be the end of difficulties.

Chapter 2

William in California Gold Country

A NOTHER FORTY-NINER WITH WHOM William Brickell would become acquainted much later in Miami was Henry E. Perrine. Perrine recorded the scene that met both men in the young city of San Francisco when they each arrived in the late fall of 1849 seeking their fortunes. Perrine wrote:

Nearly 40,000 immigrants landed in San Francisco in 1849. Three or four thousand seamen deserted from the many hundreds of ships lying in the harbor.

There was no such thing as a home to be found; scarcely even a proper house could be seen. Both dwellings and places of business were either common canvas tents or small rough board shanties or frame buildings of one story.

Only the great gambling saloons, hotels, restaurants, stores and a few public buildings had any pretension to size, comfort, or elegance.

The streets were uneven and irregular. By the continued passage of horses and drays with building material and goods during the rainy season, which commenced early and was unusually severe, the different thoroughfares were soon so cut up as to become almost impassable...Where there was a piece of vacant ground one day, the next saw it covered with half a dozen tents or shanties. Horses, mules and oxen forced their way through, across and over every obstruction in the streets, and men waded and toiled after them.[27]

Abandoned ships in San Francisco Harbor, 1849.

San Francisco Hotel, 1850.

Soon after arriving in the city, Perrine met a man with whom he had read law in Buffalo. "When I told him that I expected to try the mines he said, 'Perrine, don't do it. Stop right here and hang out your shingle.'"[28] The advice given to Perrine was a lesson William Brickell would learn and put to good use later on. Whether the miners found gold was unpredictable, but one was guaranteed to do well by going into business in gold country.

Perrine cites "some astonishing facts with regard to prices." He recorded:

> *Carpenters who were receiving twelve dollars per day* [$306 in 2008] *struck work, and after asking for sixteen dollars* [$409 in 2008], *got fourteen dollars* [$358 in 2008] *with promise of an increase; skilled mechanics received from twelve dollars to twenty dollars per day* [$306 to $511 in 2008]. *A single store rudely constructed of rough boards brought $3,000 per month* [$76,725 in 2008] *payable in advance. The Parker House yielded $10,000 a month* [$255,751 in 2008] *in rents. Eight to fifteen per cent a month was paid in advance for the use of money with real security.* [29]

Although William learned that a businessman in gold country could make a fortune without having to struggle with a pickaxe and shovel, there is no good evidence that he applied the lesson in California.

THERE ARE DIFFERING REPORTS OF HOW William spent three years in California, from November 1849 to September 1852. The writer of a biographical entry in a 1902 book, when William and Mary were alive and might have been interviewed, stated that William established a wholesale mercantile business in San Francisco.[30] Ralph Munroe, an early pioneer with whom William had a chance encounter in New York and persuaded to move to South Florida,[31] said that William told him he studied law prior to going to California and became a law partner to a famous judge in San Francisco.[32] Maude Brickell told an interviewer for a newspaper article late in life that her father became "very, very rich" in the gold fields of California, implying that he became rich digging for gold.[33] Each of these claims is questionable for a different reason.

The 1850 federal census for San Francisco has not survived, but San Francisco city directories for 1850 and 1852 do exist, and William Brickell is not listed in them. If he had established a business or become a law partner in the city during this period, it would have been to his advantage to make certain his name appeared in these directories.[34]

The only other logical place to establish a business and sell to miners during this time was in the fledgling city of Sacramento, closer to the gold fields than San Francisco. But William's name does not appear either in the 1850 federal census for Sacramento or an existing 1851 Sacramento City Directory.[35]

Since there is no evidence of William residing in either of these cities, it is most likely that he arrived in the gold fields and began digging for gold. Although his name doesn't appear in the 1850 federal census for El Dorado County, center

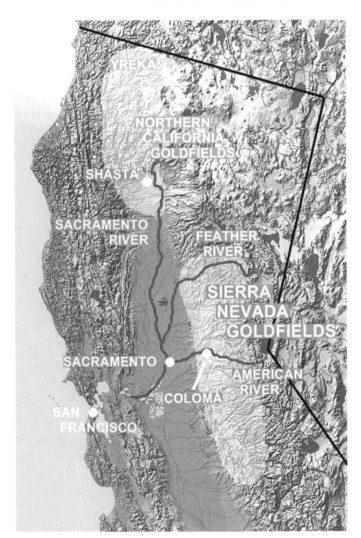

California gold fields.

of the mining activity where Sutter's Mill and the early mines and diggings were located, or in the census of surrounding mining counties, the situation in rural counties where the gold fields were located was far different from that of the cities. Census takers in 1850 couldn't be expected to track down and account for the tens of thousands of miners swarming the hills, ravines, creeks and rivers. Besides, miners wanted to keep their locations secret in case they struck it rich.

Those who sought gold in the Sierra Nevada streams, ravines and mountains endured about as much hardship in the gold fields as they had suffered getting to California. Perrine gave a sense of the experience:

It soon began to rain once more. Before we had proceeded twenty yards, one of the oxen tumbled down to rise no more. We took the few things we had in the wagon and placed them in another, which was being hauled by two oxen, and placing our five oxen before the four, they all struggled along through the mud.

We passed many wagons that had been mired and abandoned, their loads going to waste. If we attempted the side of the road we found it worse than the center, and thus we waded on through the mud and mire until we reached Green Springs about five miles farther on, losing in the meantime another one of our oxen...Very soon we came to a place where the mule we were leading went down in the mire up to his belly, and notwithstanding repeated efforts, which at times seemed almost crowned with success as he struggled to get out, he was so weak that he could not rise from the mud and we were reluctantly compelled to leave him to die.[36]

Perrine also wrote something that William undoubtedly could have written himself:

My hands were both well blistered by the use of the pick and shovel. The only water for drinking purposes we had to procure from the little stream at the bottom of the canyon, and as that was used constantly for washing gold, it was about like a mud puddle in the streets at home. Our only recourse was to take a pailful [sic] up to our camping place and leave it to settle over night; but even then it looked so dark colored with sediment that in self-defense I learned to drink coffee, which I had never drank [sic] up to that time. Boiling the water with the coffee and sweetening it served to disguise the otherwise muddy taste.[37]

In the early days of 1848 and 1849, it was not uncommon for a miner to find $2,000 of gold a day (about $50,000 in 2008). But the average miner might be lucky to find $10 per day[38] (about $250 in 2008). As for Maude's claim that her father had fantastic success in the gold fields of California, there is an indication that he probably didn't become "very, very rich" during this period.

IN 1851, GOLD WAS DISCOVERED IN Australia. By 1852, word had spread among the California miners of the new find. William joined an exodus of

Miner panning for gold, 1850.

miners who set out for the newly discovered gold fields. On September 4, 1852, he sailed from San Francisco for Sydney, Australia, aboard the five-hundred-ton steamer *Pactolus* with 170 other passengers. He was not one of 7 passengers who traveled first class on the voyage, apparently having a reason to save money by traveling in steerage.[39]

On the voyage to Sydney, William met or perhaps already knew Adam Kidd, a first-class passenger on the ship. In Australia, William would team up with Adam and indeed become "very, very rich."

Chapter 3

William Finds Wealth
in Australia

WILLIAM BRICKELL, TWENTY-SEVEN, and Adam Kidd, thirty-one, arrived in Sydney, Australia, on November 3, 1852.[40] William and Adam were both from Ohio. Possibly they had known each other in Ohio or in the gold fields of California, or perhaps they became acquainted on their two-month voyage from San Francisco. Wherever and whenever they met, their fortunes would be closely linked over the next nine and a half years.

The two men would succeed in amassing a significant fortune in Australia. What is remarkable is that they would do so in spite of Australian distrust of Americans at the time. Aussies who had flocked to the California gold rush and were loyal subjects of the British Crown sent back widely reported accounts of "mobism" that horrified their countrymen. "Californians" were gun-carrying revolutionaries who took the law into their own hands, lynching those who stole horses, ambushed gold carriers or were a problem to the miners in other ways. Australians considered themselves more civilized than this because of an authority that came from a top-down monarchy rather than from a bottom-up democracy.[41]

The extraordinary research of two Australian authors, H. Denise McMahon and Christine G. Wild, has uncovered extensive information about how William Brickell spent his time in Australia. A chapter is devoted to William in their book, *American Fever, Australian Gold: American & Canadian Involvement in Australia's Gold Rush*,[42] and they also focused on him with an article, "William Barnwell Brickell in Australia," that appeared in the 2007 issue of *Tequesta*, the journal of the Historical Association of Southern Florida.[43] Further information has emerged from e-mail exchanges that I initiated with McMahon and from my own research. As a result, we have a clear picture of how the young William became very wealthy in Australia.

WILLIAM AND ADAM ARRIVED IN SOUTHEAST Australia at Sydney, the capital of New South Wales on the Pacific Ocean. They trekked by horseback or wagon 365 miles southwest to Albury, a frontier town on the Murray River.[44] The river, the largest in Australia, is the border between the districts of New South Wales and Victoria, the capital of which is Melbourne, 186 miles farther south from Albury on the Indian Ocean. The area between Sydney and Melbourne was known as the Australian outback and had "neither facilities nor infrastructure, and until gold was discovered, little population."[45]

The terrain of the outback was similar to the gold fields of California. In fact, it was because an Australian, Edward Hargraves, had gone to California in the early days of the gold rush and had recognized the similarity of the terrain to the Australian outback, learned how to find gold in the sands of streams and rushed back home to prove a hunch that he discovered gold in Australia. His discovery was made in what would become one of Australia's richest gold fields, Bathurst, west of Sydney. Within a week of his announcement, $50,000 in gold (approximately $1,200,000 in 2008) was uncovered in the immediate area.[46]

Albury was one of only a few settlements in the outback prior to the discovery of gold. It was centrally located to the gold fields at an important crossing point on the Murray River between the two major districts of New South Wales and Victoria on the only inland road stretching from Sydney to Melbourne.

In 1852, when William and Adam reached Albury, they found only a few huts, a post office, a custom post, police barracks, a blacksmith shop, two inns and a recently established public school.[47] Before setting out for a nearby gold

Map of the Murray River, which divides New South Wales and Victoria.

Looking across the Murray River from New South Wales to Victoria.

field, they must have realized the commercial potential of Albury and how a man might make a fortune in ways other than digging for gold.

Tens of thousands of gold seekers were flooding into the Australian ports of Sydney and Melbourne. A total of 94,664 fortune hunters arrived in Melbourne alone in 1852, an average of more than 1,800 a week—more than had come to San Francisco in the first year of the California gold rush.[48] Many set out for Albury with a need for housing, food and supplies near the gold fields.

Moreover, thousands of Australians were leaving their jobs and heading in the same direction. One account stated: "Australia's economy depended on wool. The shearing season had arrived but the shearers had thrown down their blades to prospect for gold. The stevedores who customarily loaded the wool bales into ships' holds had also quit their jobs."[49] In the port of Melbourne "stood hundreds of vessels flying the flags of all nations—whalers, steamers, American clippers, emigrant ships, fine East Indiamen—all stalled for want of seamen. It was worse than San Francisco in 1849."[50]

Australia was on the verge of becoming the world's richest gold find. By 1853, the gold fields of New South Wales and Victoria would be out-producing California by millions of dollars. One Victoria area alone, Ballarat, would produce $300 million worth of gold by that date (over $7.6 billion in 2008), more than all the Sierra Nevada in California had produced in the four years since 1849. Seventy miles to the north another strike, Bendigo, would produce an even larger amount.[51]

The gold strikes in the outback were miles apart, and the ranges separating them contained some of the richest gold fields on earth. The supply seemed almost inexhaustible. Indeed, the Australian gold rush remains the world's richest to the present time.[52]

William and Adam left Albury and prospected in nearby Yackandandah, a thirty-mile valley with a rich supply of gold.[53]

In an e-mail exchange, McMahon gave an interesting bit of information about gold diggers from the United States: "Americans stuck together through business and friendship on the gold fields, celebrating their July 4, Presidents' birthdays, etc. July 4ths were big nights with speeches, singing, tales, banquets—all on the gold fields hundreds of miles from the cities or large towns."[54]

IT ISN'T KNOWN HOW LONG WILLIAM AND ADAM prospected in Yackandandah, but by early 1854 they had returned to Albury and had leased a barge to ferry those wishing to cross the Murray River from Albury to the gold fields of Victoria. "From this venture the pair made the enormous sum of £10,000."[55]

McMahon and Wild were able to learn from letters written by American miners to relatives back home that £10,000 was the equivalent of $50,000 U.S. at the time. To fully appreciate this amount, $50,000 in 1854 was equivalent to $1,184,034 in 2008. And the ferry was just the beginning of many entrepreneurial successes William and Adam would have.

In 1856, the partners both applied for and were granted British citizenship, allowing them to own property in the Australian colony.[56] Under the banner of Kidd & Brickell, they opened a huge retail and wholesale store that catered to the thousands passing through Albury. The store not only sold mining tools and supplies but also furniture, cooking utensils, lumber, building supplies, hardware, spirits, foodstuffs and clothing.[57] They were the Sam Walton of the gold fields!

All of these items had to be transported from great distances, justifying highly inflated sales prices. The first paddle steamer had come up the Murray River from South Australia in 1855, the year before William and Adam opened their store.[58] William was possibly the partner who went for the goods sold in the store, traveling downstream on the river to established towns and cities on the Indian Ocean. He knew about buying and selling; his father had operated a wholesale business in Steubenville, and before leaving for California the young William had been involved in a mercantile business of his own.

William made at least one trip back to the United States, arriving at New York on May 23, 1854, on the *Margareth Ann*.[59] He didn't stay long, returning to Sydney on October 10 on the *London*,[60] with most of the intervening months spent on the sea. Likely he would have returned with American goods that could be sold at exorbitant prices in Australia.

One report told of an American in Melbourne who profited 200 percent on a shipment of items brought from Boston. He then ordered more from that city and claimed a net profit of $95,000 the first year of his business (approximately $2,500,000 in 2008). Another American in Melbourne

Illustration of the
Exchange Hotel from
an advertisement.

established a coach service with American coaches and drivers that took miners to the Bendigo diggings. Each vehicle carried fourteen passengers inside and on top. The businessman sold out for a reported $250,000 in 1854[61] (just under $6,000,000 in 2008).

Although William's possible role as procurer and transporter for the partners was not documented by McMahon and Wild, they noted that he seemed to be the "silent partner," with Adam taking a more active role in Albury's civic affairs.[62] William's absence would explain this. When Albury was proclaimed a municipality in 1859, Adam was elected one of the first nine aldermen on the Albury Municipal Council.

In 1858, Kidd & Brickell built and opened Albury's first hotel, the Exchange. A local newspaper established in 1856, the *Albury Border Post*, bragged, "A hotel of this style has never been seen before in the district, the furniture alone costing many thousands of pounds."[63] The Exchange offered beautifully furnished rooms, a secure stable, a restaurant for dining and a bar offering wines and spirits with "English Ale and Porter kept on draught."[64]

Immediately the hotel became the center of life in Albury, a town of some one thousand people by then. Other entrepreneurs leased rooms at the Exchange and operated businesses from the hotel. Coach services used its stable.[65]

Money was flowing from the gold-rich outback. One account reported "lavish squandering by the new-rich. One man was said to have shod his horse with gold. Another lighted his cigars with £5 notes [$25 then; $615 in 2008]. A third had set up champagne bottles like tenpins for his friends to strike down."[66]

In addition to riches, William Brickell would find something more in Australia!

Chapter 4

William Meets Mary

ONE FAMILY LIVING IN THE FRONTIER TOWN of Albury in southeast Australia at the same time William Brickell was accumulating wealth was Joseph and Catherine Bulmer, their one son, Joseph Jr., and five daughters, Elizabeth, Mary, Frances, Sarah and Emily.

Joseph Sr., a carpenter, had come to Australia in 1840 from England with his wife, Catherine Merriman Bulmer, and three young children. They came as "bounty immigrants." Australia was a penal colony for the mother country. To attract immigrants other than convicts, the government offered to pay the passage for "free people" and guaranteed them a job upon arrival.[67]

The Bulmer family settled in Goulburn, a town 100 miles southwest of Sydney, where Joseph purchased several town lots in 1847 and 1851.[68] By 1855, the family had migrated another 265 miles south to Albury, where Joseph purchased land at an auction on September 17, 1855.[69]

The second-oldest daughter was a very pretty Mary who caught the eye of William Brickell. Mary was born in Little Bolton, Lancashire, England, on February 20, 1836. She was three years old when her parents migrated to Australia.

It isn't clear when she and William became a couple. In 1856, working as a dressmaker in Albury when she was twenty years old, Mary became pregnant. She went to Goulburn to have the baby, staying with her older sister, Elizabeth, and her sister's husband, John Morgan. Mary gave birth to Amy Alice Bulmer on January 5, 1857. She registered the birth in Goulburn, as required by law, left the father's name blank on the certificate and gave the baby her own last name.[70]

Presumably the father was William. He and Mary claimed this to be true in later years. But they wouldn't formally marry until five years later on May 20, 1862, in a Presbyterian church at Melbourne, sailing the next day to America as husband and wife.[71]

There is an indication that Mary was pregnant with a second daughter by the time they left Australia. Maude Brickell's biographical sketch about her parents states that a sister, Emma Stanhope Brickell, was born in Panama during her parents' trip from Australia.[72] Although Emma's place of birth is given as Panama in official records, the date of birth is stated as January 28, 1863, five months after William and Mary passed through Panama.[73]

Young Mary in Australia.

Perhaps the birth date was falsified in records to allow for a pregnancy after the marriage, thereby protecting Emma from later gossip. Perhaps for the same reason, the story of Alice's birth in Australia was falsified by William and Mary. Alice was said to have been William's daughter from an earlier marriage,[74] which wasn't true.

In an e-mail exchange with Denise McMahon, I questioned what the situation might have been in Albury in the 1850s to explain why William and Mary didn't marry there. Her reply was that in doing research, she and her partner found that many didn't feel the need to marry in a remote area such as Albury, where there was little civilization and no officialdom.[75]

For William's 1908 obituary, Mary gave their marriage date as January 1855, seven years and four months prior to their Melbourne ceremony.[76] Perhaps this was when they made a personal commitment to each other.

OTHER QUESTIONS WERE RAISED FOR ME about the death of Mary's father. According to his death certificate, Joseph Bulmer died on May 23, 1858, at the age of forty-nine from a "cold acting on a debilitated constitution."[77] But McMahon and Wild found a brief notice in the *Albury Border Post* about an inquest several months after Joseph's death stating that "intemperance" had contributed to his death.[78] In questioning McMahon about the disparity between a doctor's finding on the death certificate and that of a jury months later, McMahon gave a possible explanation:

> *This recording of a death as due to drinking was used before a study was done on colonial beer near the end of the 1880s. The study found that many deaths, which had been marked as due to drunkenness, may not necessarily have been because the man or woman was alcoholic. In the early years of settlement in Australia, beer was made under the same methods as it had been in the cold countries of England or Europe. However, due to the warmer climes of Australia, the yeasts interacted in the heat, producing fusel oil, a poison. Therefore, it was not a matter of how much was drunk in some cases, but what they drank. The study found that an inordinate number of people prior to the late 1880s had died from delirium tremens and alcoholic poisoning. Fusel oil today is used as a solvent in lacquers and enamels.[79]*

BY 1858, WILLIAM AND ADAM HAD branched out into other business ventures that brought them even more profits. They were already operating a barge service across the Murray River, a large retail and wholesale store and the Exchange Hotel with its fine rooms, stable, restaurant and bar.

Now they established a coach service from Albury to Melbourne, a distance of 186 miles, with two five-horse American wagons. Also they built a second one-hundred-room Exchange Hotel at the site of a new gold strike in a desolate area of Kiandra in the Australian Alps between Albury and Sydney.

And then the government of New South Wales decided to build a bridge across the Murray River in Albury to make the crossing into Victoria easier. Kidd & Brickell bid for the job, got it and became contractors. Their entrepreneurial spirit seemed to have no bounds!

Lastly, they leased sixteen thousand acres of land east of Albury on the other side of the Murray River in Victoria and grazed cattle.[80]

By 1862, THE UNITED STATES WAS IN the desperate throes of a Civil War, and William decided the time had come to go home. Although Adam would stay in Australia another three years, the partners began collecting outstanding debts and selling property and businesses in preparation for William's departure.

Prior to William leaving, the *Albury Border Post* printed an article on April 16, 1862, revealing that William and Adam had done more in Albury than enrich themselves. Indeed, for a decade they had been integral to the development of the town. The newspaper praised the men for providing capital to many who had started businesses and for lending money to struggling tradesmen. They had contributed generously to every charity and institutional drive over the years. The article added, "Many a public institution in Albury would have been aborted if not for the encouragement of the firm of Kidd & Brickell."[81]

On May 21, 1862, the day after William and Mary married in Melbourne, Mr. and Mrs. William Brickell and five-year-old Alice sailed for San Francisco on the *Seaman's Bride*.[82] The following day, May 22, William celebrated his thirty-seventh birthday aboard the ship. Mary was twenty-six.

They arrived in San Francisco eighty-five days later on August 14. From there they sailed to Panama, a seven-day voyage, and crossed the Isthmus by rail—available by then.[83]

There is a three-week gap in Panama before they sailed for New York from Aspinwall, located on the Atlantic coast. Presumably the delay was due to Mary giving birth to Emma, as noted in Maude's sketch.

On September 18, the family sailed for New York from Aspinwall on the *Arial*.[84]

Chapter 5

Brickells Seek a Homeplace

AFTER A FOUR-MONTH JOURNEY FROM AUSTRALIA, William and Mary Brickell, with five-year-old Alice and infant Emma, arrived in New York on September 26, 1862.[85] According to Maude's biographical sketch, the family then journeyed to Pittsburgh to visit William's cousin, David Zachariah Brickell.[86] Maude referred to David as William's uncle, but David was more likely his cousin, as he was four and a half months younger than William. As boys they would have seen a lot of each other since William was raised in Steubenville, Ohio, an unofficial suburb of Pittsburgh, and David married a young lady from Steubenville.[87]

In 1862, David was a steamboat captain, as his father John had been, and David's wife and children lived at 44 Center Avenue in Pittsburgh, where William's family would have stayed.[88] Because David's occupation was considered crucial to the interests of the Union during the Civil War, he was exempt from serving in the army.[89] In partnership with another captain, he built and ran a number of river steamers that transported Union troops and supplies during the war.[90]

By the 1860s, Pittsburgh was a great industrial center with a population of some forty thousand. The "Iron City" manufactured munitions for the Union army, from the smallest arms to the largest cannons and gunboats. Over half of the steel and one-third of the glass manufactured in the United States originated from Pittsburgh at that time.[91]

Maybe because Mary was caring for an infant and William wanted to get her away from the stress of the Civil War, he took her and the two children to California, where he had another cousin, David's brother John.[92] John

Brickell lived in Smartsville in the foothills of the Sierra Nevada Mountains in California gold country.[93] Presumably John had gone to California during the gold rush as William had done. Back in the gold fields, William was able to show Mary where he had spent three years before going to Australia.

But they didn't stay in California. According to information Mary gave for William's obituary in 1908, they "tired" of the West. William wanted to "visit his big old home in Ohio," and they returned to Steubenville.[94]

MAUDE'S SKETCH INDICATES THAT EITHER BEFORE or after going to California and returning to Steubenville, William, Mary and the children were in Washington, D.C., where Mary volunteered as a citizen nurse to care for wounded soldiers at the White House.[95] Research reveals that during the Civil War, twenties of thousands of soldiers, Union and Confederate, were brought from battlefields to be cared for in some fifty-six improvised hospitals in Washington. One of the hospitals was the Reynolds Barracks Hospital set up on what is now the south lawn of the White House.[96] Perhaps this is where Mary helped with the wounded.

In an article about Washington's Civil War hospitals, writer Alice Price described Washington at the time as "a relatively rural town with limited medical accommodations...These hospitals only added to the wartime atmosphere of the city that already swarmed with regiments of soldiers. Army wagons and artillery tore up the unpaved streets and roads, and ambulances jolted by at all hours."[97]

Price notes, "At the beginning of the war there was not a single medically trained female nurse in America...The overload of patients was so great that the physicians were simply unable to give enough individual attention to the men, [and therefore] the contributions of [citizen] nurses were inestimable."[98]

Walt Whitman, who also volunteered as a nurse in Washington, described the hospitals in a letter to his mother in 1864: "I suppose you know that what we call a hospital here in the field is nothing but a collection of tents on the bare ground for a floor."[99] In other writings he spoke of his duties, which involved the "refuse pail, soon to be filled with clotted rags and blood, emptied and filled again" and to "cleanse the one with a gnawing and putrid gangrene, so sickening, so offensive."[100]

The experience of the nurses was undoubtedly horrific. Three out of four operations were amputations.[101]

Of her own experience, Mary told Maude that during the Civil War she "did all she could do to help with sick and wounded soldiers" and "saw more blood, suffering and dying men than she had ever seen before."[102]

BY MARCH 1, 1865, THE BRICKELLS WERE back in Pennsylvania, where Mary gave birth to their first son, William Barnwell Brickell, named after his father and grandfather.

A month and a half later, on April 11, General Robert E. Lee surrendered the Confederate cause. Four days after that, on April 15, President Lincoln was assassinated. Citizens of Pittsburgh went into deep mourning for President Lincoln, who, as president-elect, had visited the city in 1861. He had told the citizens of Pittsburgh how important their industrial output would be to the Union cause.[103]

With Civil War hostilities at an end, William's cousin David, with partners, purchased an iron manufacturing company in Pittsburgh, renaming it Martin, Oliver & Brickell. David would go on to become a leading citizen of Pittsburgh. He would become a partner in the biggest glass factory in the world at the time, Chambers & McKee, which was located in Jeanette, a suburb of Pittsburgh; would serve as president of a railroad, the South Side Railway Co.; and would be a director of several banks in Pittsburgh and Jeannette.[104]

But William was interested in something else—a new industry born in 1859 with the discovery of the first oil well in western Pennsylvania by Colonel Edwin Drake. The war had held back the fledgling oil industry, which primarily provided kerosene for lighting lamps. Now with the war's end, the industry's growth exploded. Oil was shipped from the fields of western Pennsylvania by railroad to Pittsburgh to be refined in the city's fifty-eight oil refineries.[105]

Competing fiercely with Pittsburgh for the oil refining business was a city equidistant from the oil fields and located on Lake Erie, which gave it an advantage for shipping products east to the Atlantic Ocean through the Erie Canal. The city was Cleveland, Ohio.

William moved his family in late 1865 to Cleveland, where

David Z. Brickell.

Mary gave birth to three more children. On October 4, 1866, a third daughter was born, Edith Mary Kate Brickell. A year and a half later, on April 30, 1868, a second son followed, Charles Clinton B. Brickell. One year after that, on April 15, 1869, Belle Gertrude Brickell was born.

In 1867, William brought Mary's mother, Catherine Bulmer, and Mary's sister, Emily, eighteen, from Australia to Cleveland for a visit. They arrived at New York on June 24 by first-class passage aboard the *Bellance* by way of England.[106]

WILLIAM AND MARY BECAME ACQUAINTED WITH a man in Cleveland who would play a much larger role in their lives three decades later: Henry M. Flagler. The Flaglers resided at 300 Prospect and, by 1870, moved to 401 Euclid, across the street from the John D. Rockefellers at 424 Euclid. The Brickells lived some five blocks away at 167 Garden, a property they purchased for $2,600 ($36,162 in 2008) on November 11, 1865, and would sell for $6,000 ($100,962 in 2008) on November 25, 1870.[107]

The Brickells and Flaglers were both Presbyterian and would have attended the same Euclid Avenue Presbyterian Church. Flagler's father was an itinerant Presbyterian minister in New York.[108]

Another connection between the Brickells and Flagler was through business. Mary said that she saw Flagler "almost daily" when they lived in Cleveland.[109] According to a newspaper interview Maude gave in 1960, William had a successful wholesale grocery business in Cleveland.[110]

In 1866, Flagler was thirty-six years old. Heavily in debt from the failure of a Michigan salt company that collapsed after the war, he moved to Cleveland and went into the grain business. Rockefeller, twenty-seven, was a partner in a grain and produce company in Cleveland, Rockefeller & Clark. Flagler made consignments to Rockefeller.[111] William would have had business dealings with both men through a wholesale grocery business.

Before forming Rockefeller & Clark with partner M.B. Clark, Rockefeller had worked as a bookkeeper and clerk for commission merchants Hewitt & Tuttle. The Tuttle was the father-in-law of another Cleveland resident, Julia Sturtevant Tuttle, who also would play a large role in the Brickells' lives three decades later.

Rockefeller & Clark profited tremendously during the Civil War by selling produce to the Federal government. The partners expanded their interests by joining with a third partner, Samuel Andrews, and establishing an oil refining company, Andrews, Clark & Co. After the war, Rockefeller bought out Clark, sold his produce interests and focused on the oil business, forming Rockefeller & Andrews.[112]

Henry M. Flagler.

In 1867, the oil industry was growing rapidly with the spreading use of kerosene for lighting. Rockefeller was looking for capital to expand his business.[113] He approached Flagler for money. Flagler borrowed $100,000 (just under $1.5 million in 2008) from his wife's family and became a principal owner in the renamed firm of Rockefeller, Andrews & Flagler.[114]

A wealthy William, now forty-two years old, also had money to invest. According to Maude's biographical sketch, he lent "these two young fellows"—Rockefeller, fourteen years younger, and Flagler, five years younger—"money to pay taxes on 375 acres of oil land." She implies that Rockefeller and Flagler sold the land for taxes and used William's money to buy other land that they put in their own names, and William never profited from the transaction or got his money back.[115]

Rockefeller was known for his bargaining and borrowing skills. "John always got the best of the bargain," Cleveland men said.[116] Moreover, he could

John D. Rockefeller.

borrow as well as bargain. Growing as it was, the firm's capital was limited. It often needed money. Rockefeller's partner bragged, "Oh, he was the greatest borrower you ever saw!"[117]

By 1868, rampant speculation had overbuilt the oil industry. Refining capacity far outpaced crude production. There were twenty-six refineries in Cleveland alone.[118] Prices fluctuated dramatically. Rockefeller believed that 90 percent of the refineries were operating in the red. Flagler came up with an idea to absorb the other refineries by buying them out and, if they wouldn't sell, driving them out of business by getting secret rebates from railroad companies—which Rockefeller was said to be a genius at negotiating—and underselling them.[119] It was a scheme that would be referred to as the "Cleveland Massacre."[120]

Ida Tarbell, in her serialized and widely read 1904 classic, "The History of the Standard Oil Company," which motivated President Theodore Roosevelt to take on the monopolies in the early twentieth century, described their tactics: "They fought their way to control by rebate and drawback, bribe and blackmail, espionage and price cutting."[121]

Of Flagler Tarbell said, "He had no scruples to make him hesitate over the ethical quality of a contract which was advantageous. Success, that is making money, was its own justification."[122] William would learn more of Flagler's tactics decades later.

Rockefeller escorts his sister-in-law Lucy Spelman through the East Cleveland railway station.

Rockefeller and Flagler put all other Cleveland refineries out of business in an amazingly short amount of time. It is said that within one forty-eight-hour period alone Rockefeller intimidated six refineries to sell out, some at ten cents on the dollar.[123]

One owner of a competing refinery, John H. Alexander, explained how the coup succeeded: "There was a pressure brought to bear upon my mind and upon almost all citizens of Cleveland engaged in the oil business...that if we did not sell out we should be crushed out...It was said that they had a contract with railroads by which they could run us into the ground."[124]

In 1870, Rockefeller, Flagler and three other associates formed the Standard Oil Company. By 1878, Standard Oil controlled 90 percent of all oil refineries in the United States.[125]

Oby Bonawit, in his 1980 book, *Miami, Florida: Early Families & Records*, states that William "prospered in oil" in Ohio.[126] And a 1966 article by Agnes

Ash in the *Miami News* claimed, "Brickell made a lot of money until, so the story goes, John D. Rockefeller squeezed him out."[127]

If William invested in an oil refinery in Cleveland that at first did well but then was a victim of the "Cleveland Massacre," it would explain residual tension between William and Flagler that would surface three decades later.

Along with whatever unpleasant experiences William had regarding Flagler and Rockefeller with a loan and possible oil investment gone bad, William may have been burned out on Cleveland as a result of other unhappy dealings. He commissioned a wood manufacturer to build a hat rack for him. He claimed that the manufacturer, Henry Beilstein, didn't build the hat rack according to his instructions. William refused to pay the agreed-upon $450 price and offered instead to take the hat rack for $150. Beilstein refused and, on June 6, 1867, filed a complaint in the Court of Common Pleas suing William for $450 with interest. A jury awarded Beilstein a $466 judgment. William appealed the case, heard in February 1868, but only succeeded in getting the judgment reduced to $450.50.[128]

WILLIAM HAD BEGUN LOOKING FOR A WAY out of Cleveland. According to Maude, Mary didn't like the cold weather and wanted to move to the kind of temperate climate she had enjoyed in Australia.[129]

On January 30, 1867, William responded to an advertisement offering a plantation for sale in Georgia. He wrote a letter to the owner, W.H. Branch, asking: "What will be your lowest price in four installments commencing January 1, 1868? You will please inform me as to improvements and what amount of land is under cultivation with the several kinds of production."[130] He went on to express his desire to examine the plantation upon a response from Branch. In the end, either the plantation or the offer wasn't acceptable.

William then learned of a woman at Columbia, South Carolina, Harriet English, who wanted to sell four large land tracts at the southern tip of Florida that she had inherited from her deceased son, William English. Three of the tracts were on Biscayne Bay at what would become Miami, and another was twenty-six miles up the coast at New River, which would become Fort Lauderdale.

William invited Julia Tuttle's father, Ephraim T. Sturtevant, a sixty-seven-year-old retired schoolteacher who lived on a farm in East Cleveland, to go with him to explore the land. Sturtevant agreed to go. Like Mary, Sturtevant did not like the cold weather and sought a warmer climate to live out his last years.[131]

In March 1870, William and Sturtevant traveled by railroad to North Florida. There they chartered a small vessel and made a tour of the southern portion of the peninsula, where they found a vast semitropical wilderness with astonishing natural beauty and a balmy, sunny temperature.[132]

A naturalist who visited Biscayne Bay four years later described the beauty:

Wild fowl and fish abound in numbers I have never seen equaled in any other part of the world. Three hundred and fifty varieties of birds have been already found in Florida...Flowers covered the ground and hung in brilliant festoons from the trees, while flowering shrubs of rare and beautiful species clothed the banks of every little stream and formed a dense undergrowth in the wooded river bottoms.[133]

Only twelve white families were scattered throughout a vast wilderness along a fifty-mile-long Biscayne Bay. A remnant of Seminole Indians lived on islands in the nearby Everglades.[134] It was a little-known paradise.

The choice location for a homesite was at the mouth of the Miami River where it flowed into Biscayne Bay. Both William and Sturtevant decided this was where they wanted to live.

William visited Mrs. English at Columbia and learned that the title to her land grants was not clear. Mrs. English gave him a power of attorney, dated June 24, 1870, to foreclose on any mortgages, pay or settle any taxes due and clear up any other title encumbrances on her property in Dade County.[135] Also, William would need to get a U.S. government patent for the land, which had never been issued. He would succeed in getting it on November 19, 1872.[136]

In addition to a power of attorney, Mrs. English gave a written agreement to sell the property to William that allowed him to begin residing on the land.[137] Finally, on February 25, 1874, he was able to purchase in Mary's name the four tracts from Mrs. English. Three of the tracts—the Rebecca Hagan (Egan)[138] Donation of 620.66 acres, the Polly Lewis Donation of 634.17 acres and the Jonathan Lewis Donation of 613 acres—stretched south from the mouth of the Miami River to what would become Coconut Grove. The fourth "donation," a word used for land grant, was the Frankie Lewis Donation consisting of 640 acres located at New River (to become Fort Lauderdale). William paid $3,500 (approximately $66,000 in 2008) for a total of 2,507.83 acres.[139]

On January 12, 1871, William and Sturtevant returned to Biscayne Bay on a chartered schooner from New York with Mrs. Sturtevant, her household goods, two carpenters hired by William and enough lumber and building materials for two houses.[140]

Mary and the children would follow later.

Chapter 6

Miami as a Wilderness

A new country seems to follow a pattern. First come the openers, strong and brave and rather childlike. They can take care of themselves in a wilderness, but they are naïve and helpless against men, and perhaps that is why they went out in the first place. When the rough edges are worn off the new land, businessmen and lawyers come in to help with the development— to solve problems of ownership...And finally comes the culture, which is entertainment, relaxation, transport out of the pain of living.
—*John Steinbeck,* East of Eden

T HE CARPENTERS WILLIAM BROUGHT WITH him to Biscayne Bay completed a comfortable, two-story wood-frame house on the south bank at the mouth of the Miami River, ever after to be known as Brickell Point, and William returned to Cleveland to bring Mary and the children to their new home.

On December 9, 1871, the family sailed into the entrance of the Miami River with its waving coconut palms on a chartered schooner from New York. With them were their household effects, a housekeeper and a governess for the children. William was forty-six, Mary thirty-five, Alice fourteen, Emma eight, William Jr. six, Edith five, Charles three and Belle two.

Tragically, little Emma died of spinal meningitis on April 3, 1874. On the same day, Mary gave birth to Maudenella (later changed to Maude E. by lawyers),[141] possibly a premature birth brought on by Mary's grief. Emma was a special favorite of William. It is said that she called for him to the end, and the burial was delayed until he returned from a business trip to Key West.[142]

An early view of Brickell Point across the mouth of the Miami River.

Maude's birth year has often been erroneously cited as April 3, 1871, even on her crypt at Woodlawn Cemetery.[143] An April 3, 1874 diary entry by George Parsons, an early visitor to the Miami area, notes Maude's birth on this day and year,[144] and the 1880 federal census for Dade County correctly states Maude's age as six in 1880.[145] Maude was born the same day that her sister Emma died, and the cemetery has Emma's date of death correct as April 3, 1874.[146]

The Brickell family would be complete with the birth of a third son, George M. Brickell, in July 1878.

Mary had to be impressed with the comfortable home William had built, and he had done so under difficult circumstances. From what Maude wrote in her sketch, the lumber and materials her father and Sturtevant had brought with them eleven months earlier "was constantly stolen [and] he had to keep making replacements."[147] As a result, not enough supplies were left over to complete a house for the Sturtevants, causing hard feelings between the friends.

Sturtevant filed a $2,970 lien ($52,773 in 2008) against William's property on December 23, 1871, for "labor and materials" that he thought were due him, but he never collected.[148] In the spring of 1872, Mr. and Mrs. Sturtevant left to homestead 160 acres at the upper end of Biscayne Bay, today's Miami Shores.[149] Later, the rift between the two men would take a political turn and grow wider.

The first Brickell home at Brickell Point.

Mary settled into the Brickell home and began improving the grounds. A visitor three years later would write, "Overlooking the bay stands a house... well situated on a bluff with gardens and terraces, carefully kept and planted, making it about the prettiest residence in South Florida and the only one with any claim to taste in the laying out of the grounds."[150]

William had a small building constructed near their home for a trading post to provide food staples and other goods to the few scattered settlers in the area and to Seminole Indians who lived on islands in the vast Everglades beyond waterfalls four miles up the river. The trading post was so successful that in 1884 William constructed a much larger building, as well as a two-story warehouse with open porches and second-floor rooms to accommodate visitors.

THE SEMINOLE INDIANS WERE A REMNANT of the Creek Confederation that came to Florida at least as early as the eighteenth century from Georgia and Alabama. The word "Seminole" means "runaway" or "those that live apart."[151] When white settlers wanted their land, the U.S. Army was ordered to remove

Brickell Warehouse with second-floor guest rooms.

them to reservations west of the Mississippi River. Three wars were fought between 1817 and 1858, at the end of which 90 percent of the Seminoles had been killed or removed to Oklahoma. Remaining in the 1870s were two to four hundred individuals who had faded into the Everglades and the Big Cypress Swamp.[152] They were the only Native Americans never conquered by the United States Army.

When the Brickells settled at the mouth of the Miami River, only thirteen years had passed since the end of the third Seminole war. In the past there had been massacres of whites, and no one knew if and when the Indians might go on a rampage again.

Although other Miami settlers complained to the commissioner of Indian Affairs in Washington that they wanted the remaining Seminoles removed to the Indian Territory,[153] William and Mary made friends with them.[154] The Brickell trading post gave the Indians a way to interact peacefully with the whites while benefiting economically, and William was fair with them. He gave them gold and silver coins for their pelts, egret plumes, deer skins, alligator hides, pumpkins and sweet potatoes and sold them flour and other

Seminole Indians in the Everglades.

food staples along with beads, calico prints and hand-cranked sewing machines to make the turbans, colorful shirts and dresses they wore. When Seminoles poled their dugout cypress canoes down the river to Brickell Point, William and Mary allowed them to sleep on their porch and camp in the yard.

A settler recalled, "It was nothing in those days to see 50 or 75 Indians come...down the river along about sunset. They'd spread out their blankets on the Brickell lawn and settle down for the night. Next day they did their swapping and headed back up the river again."[155]

A yellow fever epidemic occurred in the summer of 1873. Mary put to use the nursing experience she had gained during the Civil War by turning their home into a hospital and caring for both Indians and settlers alike.[156]

William also took actions on behalf of the Seminoles. Once, when the Indians believed a venison they had left overnight with the keeper of a house of refuge near New River had been poisoned, causing sickness and death among the tribe when it was eaten, William wrote a letter to Washington reporting the incident and demanding that the alleged abuse be investigated.[157] The Indians called William their "White Chief" and Mary their "Sister."[158]

But before such trust developed, Maude relates an incident in her sketch that is consistent with reports of disquiet among the Seminoles in the early 1870s. Dr. Harry A. Kersey Jr., who did extensive research about the relationship between the Seminoles and settlers for his book *Pelts, Plumes, and Hides*, noted that in 1872 the federal government considered sending a special agent to Florida to check on reports of unrest among the Seminoles.[159] A year later, in 1873, word spread that the Seminoles were planning a revolt and were going to kill the whites. Panic spread among the settlers, and they prepared to abandon their homes and leave the area.[160] Although the report turned out to be false, unease continued between settlers and Indians.

Then, according to Maude's sketch, soon after her birth in 1874, "the Indians were expected to go on a rampage...Indians from all over Florida met...south of the Brickell home...Mrs. Brickell, with Maude, a tiny infant in her arms, went out and met the Indian Chief Big Tom Tiger and talked to him and explained to them [that] Mr. Brickell was away and she was alone with the children. After a lengthy conversation, the chief promised Mrs. B. to go away and never return in a war against the whites. They never fought again."[161]

The sketch continues, "Maude Brickell was rocked and petted by all the important Indians of her time. She was the first white baby that many of the Indians had ever seen. The Indians became staunch friends of the Brickells, coming to their home for food, medical attention and advice."[162]

SETTLERS IN THE 1870s AND 1880s WERE primarily squatters who lived in small huts or palmetto shacks scattered about the woodlands. They hunted and fished and eked out a subsistence living by manufacturing starch, similar to arrowroot, from "comptie root" that grew wild in pineland adjacent to the bay. The starch, which was used as a thickener for puddings and gravies, as a flour substitute in cookies and bread and even for starching clothes, was sold either to William or in Key West for provisions of food and clothing.

The only other local industry at the time was "wrecking," a term used for salvaging and selling the cargo of ships that were wrecked on coral reefs in the shallow waters of the bay and keys.

Maude recalled help given by her parents to the settlers. "Early schooling [of the Brickell children] was received from governesses that were employed by Mrs. Brickell, and children in the neighborhood were invited to come free of charge. The southwest room of the house was the post office, and Miss Alice was the first postmistress. The first church was held in the Brickell home."[163] Alice Brickell also taught school without pay for the 1889–90 term at Lemon City, a settlement on Biscayne Bay, until a professional teacher could be brought in.[164]

Between 1885 and 1892, the mail had to come from Palm Beach, sixty-eight miles away. There was no road, and a "barefoot mailman" came once a week to

Brickell Point by rowboat and a three-day walk along the bay shore, going without shoes so he could walk on the firm sand along the water's edge.[165]

HAVING NO FORM OF entertainment in the isolated settlement, William apparently took it upon himself to provide amusement to those who visited his trading post by spinning tall tales based on his prior adventures. William's listeners had different reactions to his yarns, one describing them as "marvelous stories" that were told "with such an air of candor that it commanded admiration for his monumental cheek."[166] Another wrote in a diary, "Mr. Brickell...entertains us with vivid accounts of his [travels]."[167]

Alice Brickell, postmistress, teacher.

A visitor recorded in his journal, "I have often regretted...not having taken notes each day of those wonderful adventures, for there was enough material furnished to have made as readable a book as the Arabian Nights."[168]

On the other hand, another member of William's audience recorded in his diary that he "got disgusted and beat a retreat."[169] Yet another branded William "the most unmitigated liar I ever knew."[170]

> *The difference between a lie and a story is that a story utilizes the trappings and appearance of truth for the interest of the listener as well as of the teller. A story has in it neither gain nor loss. But a lie is a device for profit or escape.*
>
> —*John Steinbeck,* East of Eden

William was a colorful storyteller, and at least some of his tales were truthful. He told of hunting buffalo on the plains.[171] We know this was true because a buffalo hunt was recorded in the journal of one of the young men

An Australian emu.

with William's wagon train that crossed the plains to the California gold rush. William told of living in Australia and chasing a young emu bird twenty miles on horseback before finally capturing it.[172] According to the *Encyclopaedia Britannica*, an emu is the second-largest bird in the world that can reach six feet, six inches in height and sprint thirty-one miles per hour.[173] William did live in Australia, and he could have chased the amazing native bird on horseback.

But William undoubtedly told some whoppers. According to some of his listeners, he not only chased an emu but also saw a tame one gobble up the contents of a keg of ten-penny nails weighing 112 pounds.[174] He bought an Indian shawl for $50,000 and gave it as a gift to Queen Victoria.[175] One of his fishing exploits consisted of having caught one hundred speckled trout in forty minutes, many weighing 12 pounds each, with him baiting the hook for his little boy and taking off the fish.[176]

William's storytelling sometimes got him into trouble, especially when he aired grievances against neighbors. He accused Charles Peacock of stealing a boat. Not long after that, Edgar Baker testified in court that Peacock offered him $100 "to go over the river and kill William B. Brickell." Baker replied that he "preferred making money in some other way."[177]

But William's most vehement tirades were aimed at carpetbaggers.

Chapter 7

Politics and Routine Living

WILLIAM BRICKELL WAS WELL KNOWN for his outspokenness, never mincing words when he believed an injustice had been committed. His most heated rants were targeted at carpetbaggers who, during the Reconstruction era following the Civil War, settled in the Biscayne Bay area, stole the county's elections and appointed themselves to all of the county offices.

The lead carpetbagger was William H. Gleason, a man from Wisconsin who came to Biscayne Bay in 1866 and was well entrenched in Dade County politics by the time William and Ephraim Sturtevant arrived in 1871. Sturtevant, after his falling out with William, became a neighbor and ally of Gleason farther up Biscayne Bay.

Under the Reconstruction constitution, the governor appointed all public officials, and Gleason was the Republican governor's man in Dade County.[178] Gleason's exploits are well documented in Miami's colorful early history.

Gleason, with two of his employees, William H. Hunt and a black man, Andrew Price, whom one settler said "could not write his own name,"[179] and Sturtevant dominated the Dade County Commission and all county offices. Gleason handpicked Hunt, Price, Sturtevant and another ally for the commission, which levied taxes and determined the laws of the county.[180]

In her book *Biscayne Country, 1870–1926*, Dr. Thelma Peters enumerated the county offices held by Gleason and his cohorts during the Gleason era, 1868–76. Though the offices were not held all at the same time, Gleason was circuit clerk, county clerk, tax assessor, tax collector, member of the school board (there were no schools at the time)[181] and a member of the state House of Representatives. Hunt was county commissioner, superintendent

William H. Gleason.

of schools and state senator. Sturtevant was county judge, superintendent of schools, county commissioner and state senator. Price was county commissioner and a member of the school board.[182]

Along with power, there was money to be gained. Peters gave an example of Gleason's shenanigans: "Gleason and Hunt got land through delinquent taxes. In 1872 as tax collector, Gleason sold at auction on the courthouse steps [a home on Gleason's homestead] almost 30,000 acres for which taxes were overdue. The high bidder was Hunt."[183]

In other dealings, historian Arva Moore Parks reported that Gleason's company acquired 1.35 million acres of Florida "swamp and overflow" land for six cents an acre.[184]

WILLIAM BRICKELL AND OTHER SETTLERS SOUGHT to break Gleason's stranglehold on Dade County. When election time rolled around every two years, there was high drama. One day before the 1872 election, Gleason's stacked county commission disqualified from voting William Wagner, a known anti-Gleason man, "as he did not appear before the county clerk or his deputy and take the required oath of registration."[185] One vote was important, as there were only thirty registered voters in the entire county, which at that time included today's Dade, Broward, Palm Beach and part of Martin Counties.

Two candidates were on the ballot for the state Senate, Sturtevant and Israel W. Stewart, and two for the state House of Representatives, Gleason and J.J. Brown. Stewart and Brown got the most votes, but Sturtevant and Gleason ended up in Tallahassee. Sturtevant, who illegally was an election inspector as well as a candidate,[186] threw out the ballots of three men known to have voted for Brown and Stewart. This gave Sturtevant and Gleason a one-vote victory in Dade.

But throwing out votes in Dade wasn't enough to elect Sturtevant to the Senate, as the seat represented Dade and Brevard Counties combined. Brevard had given all its votes to Stewart, who resided in the area. Gleason used his influence in Tallahassee to get the entire Brevard vote thrown out, claiming irregularities. When a review was ordered of the vote count by the state legislature, Sturtevant put on his county judge's hat, which automatically made him part of the canvassing board conducting the review, and wrote a finding that upheld the Brevard vote disqualification, securing the state Senate seat for himself.[187]

AFTER THE STEALING OF THE 1872 ELECTION, William Brickell made it his mission to break the power of Gleason and company. By 1874, his tirades had fired up enough "antis" to mount a fierce opposition to Gleason's control. A meeting was held to select candidates for county offices, and the antis were determined to make their voices heard.

Ralph Munroe, who had just moved to the settlement from New York, attended the meeting and was given a taste of the very different environment he had chosen for his new homeplace: "Shortly after our arrival at Brickell's, there was held on his place a meeting of the Dade County commissioners and we were invited to attend. As commissioners and others began arriving on boats and canoes, we noticed that many of them were armed to the teeth."[188]

Although there was no bloodshed, tempers flared. William agreed to place his name on the ballot for state representative against Gleason's candidate, W.W. Hicks.

Rose Wagner, whose father had been disqualified from voting in 1872, recalled the election in her memoirs:

> Mr. W.B. Brickell was selected by his friends as being the most worthy to represent the people of our county at this time, while there were others equally anxious to have Mr. W.W. Hicks be our next representative...One of [Hicks's] most anxious supporters was Mr. W.H. Gleason, who for the first time in years was not a candidate for any office outside of the ones he was occupying in our county, which were county clerk, assessor, and collector, besides being legal adviser for all the others.[189]

On October 4, one month before the November 3 election with Brickell and Hicks on the ballot, Gleason seized William's yacht "for taxes." Then, on October 30, three days before the voting, the commissioners purged William

Painting of William Barnwell Brickell.

from the list of qualified voters, claiming that he had "renounced his allegiance to the United States."[190] William had a dual U.S. and British citizenship from having lived in Australia. Presumably this was used as grounds for the disqualification. He was not allowed to vote in the election even though his name was on the ballot. Gleason managed to get Hicks elected by a close vote, but the gauntlet had been thrown down by the "antis."

Two years later, in 1876, Democrats prevailed in Dade with "deadly weapons in evidence."[191] Moreover, a Democratic governor and a Democratic legislature were elected in Florida. With Democrats now in power, carpetbag rule came to an end in the state.[192]

Stewart, who was elected to the Senate in the 1876 election, died before he could take office in Tallahassee. Gleason, as Dade County judge, called a secret election that only Republicans knew about and got himself elected senator in Stewart's place. The new Democratically controlled legislature in Tallahassee refused to seat him, however, and Brown, who had been cheated out of a win in 1872, replaced the deceased Stewart.[193]

In Dade, the Gleason-controlled county commission was replaced in a special election by William and three other anti-Gleason citizens.[194] William served on the commission for two years, becoming its chairman the second year.[195]

AFTER THE CARPETBAGGERS LOST POWER, life in Dade settled into a comfortable routine of work and play. William's favorite pastime was sailing. There were no roads in South Florida, and all traffic between settlements was by boat. In 1873, William bought an eleven-ton schooner in New York that he named *Ada* after his deceased mother, Adelaide Stanhope Brickell. Rose Wagner told about the sloop:

> *Mr. W.B. Brickell, having been north, returned with the yacht "Ada," purchased by him from the Brooklyn N.Y. Yacht Club. This*

A sailboat in the same class with *Ada*.

fine boat had been a prizewinner, and of her and her trophies for speed Miami's people could well be proud. Soon after her arrival and when yet in full dress for a trial of speed, she made the unbroken record of time from Key West to Miami from sun to sun.[196]

According to Munroe, also a boat enthusiast who had settled at Coconut Grove south of Miami, "Many a tax-bill that threatened [Brickell's] land was met by a turtling-trip on *Ada*, manned by his sons Will and Charles and his daughter Edith."[197] The "turtling trips" were to seize green turtles that were plentiful around the bay and could be sold in Key West.

In February 1887, Munroe, William and other boat owners decided that there were enough sailing ships in the area to organize a Biscayne Bay Yacht Club and an annual Biscayne Bay Regatta to be held on Washington's birthday. Captain Brickell was one of the club's fourteen charter members, and in the first regatta his *Ada* placed first in its class of vessels—those exceeding thirty-five feet. The annual regattas and Washington's birthday chowder parties of the Biscayne Bay Yacht Club became Dade County traditions.[198]

William was often away from home on the *Ada*, leaving Mary to run the trading post. He bought stock in New York for the trading post, either sailing there on his yacht or having the goods shipped to Key West by steamer and then bringing them to Brickell Point on the *Ada*.[199] Also, according to one writer, "Once a year he would [sail] his yacht to Boston where it would be loaded with delicacies and luxurious home furnishing accessories purchased at the most elegant store, Park & Tilford."[200]

YOUNG PEOPLE AS WELL AS ADULTS enjoyed themselves during these relaxed years. Maude recalls in her sketch, "The social life in the early days was simple but lots of fun—dancing, suppers, swimming, things that all young [people enjoy]."[201]

Mary developed the grounds around the Brickell home into a spectacular site. One visitor described how it looked in 1891:

A solid wall of magnificent cocoanut trees, intermingled with luxuriant oleanders that shot their crimson and pink blossoms thirty feet in the air, edged the banks; and through the trees beyond could be seen the large white mansion of the owner [Brickell], and to the right the storehouses and other buildings. Several small boats were drawn up to the wharf.[202]

The visitor goes on to describe that from the wharf to the trading post was a "winding, foot-worn path, which ended in a long, wide avenue that turned sharply toward the building...Overhead, the cocoanuts mingled in broad shadowy arches of interlacing leaves. Under [one's] feet the southern grass covered the coral treasury beneath, and vines and flowers of many clinging tendrils and brilliant hues gracefully festooned their hardier supports, while in the distance shimmered the waters of the beautiful Miami."[203]

In 1891, William, Mary and daughter Belle, twenty-two years old, traveled to Australia. They traveled from London in first-class cabins on the *Britannia*, arriving at Sydney on April 20, 1891.[204] Mary's mother, brother, three sisters and their families still lived in Australia. Joe Jr., fifty, was a "builder" and owned an "extensive timber-yard" in Albury, "as well as a machine shop for dressing building materials."[205]

Maude Brickell.

But routine living in the scattered settlements of Biscayne Bay was about to come to an end. Indeed, big excitement lay ahead!

Chapter 8

William's Prophecy

WILLIAM BRICKELL PROPHESIED FROM the time he and Mary settled at the mouth of the Miami River in 1871 that a railroad would come to their wilderness. Ralph Munroe remembered the "incredulous smiles" William would receive when, as early as 1877, he was predicting the arrival of a railroad.

Munroe wrote, "It was not even suggested by anyone but the 'visionary' Brickell. He would hold out his hand and say impressively, 'Mr. Monroe' (he would have it <u>Mon</u>, strongly accented), 'you will live to hear the whistle of the locomotive here.'"[206]

In anticipation of the inevitable railroad, in the late 1880s Mary began adding to the 2,507.83 acres she and William had acquired in 1874 from Harriet English. By the mid-1890s, they owned at least 6,427 acres of prime South Florida real estate—approximately 2,000 south of the Miami River, 400 at upper Biscayne Bay, 4,000 at New River (to become Fort Lauderdale) and 125 at Palm Beach.[207]

The jewel of their holdings was the Miami acreage, an unbroken tract of lush hammock that extended from the mouth of the Miami River three miles southward to Coconut Grove. The tract included a rocky bluff fronting Biscayne Bay that was the best building site in the area and the location of the "Punch Bowl," a spring in a natural rock basin that locals believed to be "the fountain of youth" that Ponce de Leon had sought when he discovered Biscayne Bay in 1513.[208]

The Brickells were biding their time awaiting the railroad. And it would be people they had known in Cleveland who, along with their own efforts, would make a railroad to the wilderness of Miami possible.

IN 1890, JULIA
TUTTLE PURCHASED
A 640-ACRE tract
from Joseph H. Day
and Messrs. Bailey and
Ford, located across the
Miami River from the
Brickells. The property
contained two stone
structures begun in
the late 1840s for an
intended plantation
by William English,
an early owner of the
property. The buildings
were completed by the
U.S. Army in 1849 for
the establishment of
Fort Dallas.[209] Julia
intended to convert one
of the structures used as
officers' quarters into a
comfortable home.

On November 13,
1891, she arrived to
take possession of
the property with her
grown children, Harry
and Fanny, household

Road through Brickell hammock to Coconut Grove.

items, a manservant, a housekeeper and a herd of
Jersey cows.

Like William, Julia had a vision of a railroad coming to Miami. After
purchasing her Miami tract, she met James E. Ingraham at a dinner party at
her Cleveland home when he was in the employ of Henry Plant, owner of
a railroad company with a terminus in Tampa on Florida's west coast. With
plans already underway to move to Miami, Julia explored with Ingraham the
possibility of Plant bringing a railroad there. She said famously to him that
evening: "Some day someone will build a railroad to Miami and I will give to
the company that does so one-half of my property at Miami for a town site.
Perhaps you will be the man."[210]

Julia Sturtevant Tuttle.

Ingraham explored the possibility of extending Plant's railroad from Tampa to Miami through the Everglades but found it to be an impractical idea. He concluded that the logical route to Miami would be down the east coast of the state. Fortuitously, he was hired away from Plant by Henry Flagler, who was in the process of extending a railroad line down the east coast and building a chain of hotels along the route.

Julia either had not known Flagler in Cleveland or had not known him well, and she wanted to be introduced to him. She contacted his Standard Oil partner, John D. Rockefeller, whom she knew from having attended the same Baptist church in Cleveland. Earlier, Julia had asked Rockefeller to recommend her to Flagler for the position of housekeeper at his new Ponce de Leon Hotel in St. Augustine. Rockefeller had inquired on her behalf, but the position was filled. She now asked Rockefeller to introduce her to Flagler, and he did so in New York City.

Henry Flagler had accumulated great wealth from his partnership with Rockefeller. He and his wife were living in New York, and she became ill. He took her to the warmer climate of Jacksonville for the winter of 1878 and was impressed with Florida's temperate climate. Following his wife's death in 1881, Flagler remarried and took his second wife to St. Augustine for their honeymoon. This time he was even more smitten by Florida, and he saw great financial potential for building a railroad and hotels at intermittent locations down the east coast to attract and accommodate wealthy vacationers from colder climates.

He purchased two short-line railroads that terminated at St. Augustine and built the luxurious Ponce de Leon Hotel there, completing it in 1885. The hotel was so successful that he built a second hotel, the Alcazar, to handle its overflow of guests. The hotels were considered the best in the world at that time.[211]

With the success of St. Augustine, Flagler began pushing his railroad south, receiving grants of land for doing so from the state, private parties and a canal company with which he entered into a partnership. He laid out town sites at intervals where he built railway stations, put in water, gas and electric facilities and even constructed houses, schools and churches—"literally building towns and cities as he went."[212]

His company advertised the attractiveness of Florida for both vacations and real estate speculation by distributing booklets, pamphlets and a magazine, the Florida east coast *Homeseeker*, throughout the United States.

WITH FLAGLER'S ANNOUNCEMENT THAT HIS RAILROAD would be extended to Palm Beach, only sixty-six miles north of Miami, Julia wrote a letter to him on November 14, 1892, offering half her land for a town site if he would bring the railroad to Miami, lay out the town and build a hotel there.[213]

In his response of April 27, 1893, Flagler turned down Julia's proposal but added a teaser: "I am very reluctant to send you an affirmative answer to your proposal; on the other hand I am almost as reluctant to decline it, for, if my life and health are spared, it seems to me more than probable that I will extend the road to Miami within a very few years."[214]

Julia followed up the exchange with a personal visit seeking to convince Flagler of the uniqueness of the Biscayne Bay climate and its potential

James E. Ingraham.

for a thriving citrus industry. But Flagler's focus was on completing his railroad and hotel at Palm Beach, and Julia returned home without further encouragement.

Actually, the wily Flagler already had interest in extending his railroad to Biscayne Bay. In the early 1890s, he had traveled incognito more than once to Lemon City, a settlement on the upper bay, to explore the possibility of bringing his railroad to that location.[215] He didn't think the Miami settlement farther south would ever be anything more than a "fishing village."[216]

In 1894, the railroad reached Palm Beach and the extravagant Royal Poinciana Hotel opened. At the time, the hotel was the largest wooden structure in the world with 1,150 rooms.[217] As with the Ponce de Leon in St. Augustine, the Royal Poinciana was an immediate success with wealthy visitors flocking to Palm Beach from the North.

Then in the winter of 1894–95, a severe freeze hit Florida and wiped out its orange groves, the principal industry in the state as well as Flagler's primary source of railway freight business. Palm Beach had escaped the devastating effects of a first freeze on December 24 and an even worse freeze four days later, but its fruit and vegetables couldn't survive temperatures that dropped into the teens on February 8.[218] It was a disaster for the state of Florida.

Ingraham immediately traveled to Miami on an inspection trip. He was excited to find orange and other fruit trees unharmed and vegetables growing undisturbed.

Although Julia Tuttle is given credit for what followed, Ingraham later gave an account of the facts and his role in them in a speech to the Miami Woman's Club:

> *I gathered up a lot of blooms from these various trees, put them in damp cotton, and after an interview with Mrs. Tuttle and Mr. and Mrs. Brickell of Miami, I hurried to St. Augustine where I called on Mr. Flagler and showed him the orange blossoms, telling him that I believed these orange blossoms were from the only part of Florida, except possibly a small area on the extreme southerly part of the western coast, which had escaped the freeze; that here was a body of land more than 40 miles long, between the Everglades and the Atlantic Ocean, absolutely untouched, and that I believed it would be the home of the citrus industry in the future because it was absolutely immune from devastating freeze. I said, "I have also here written proposals from Mrs. Tuttle and Mr. and Mrs. Brickell inviting you to extend your railroad from Palm Beach to Miami*

and offering to share with you their holdings at Miami for a town site." Mr. Flagler looked at me for some minutes in perfect silence, then he said: "How soon can you arrange for me to go to Miami?"[219]

In a 1949 *Tequesta* article, J.K. Dorn gives an account of Flagler's subsequent trip:

Mr. Flagler, Mr. Ingraham, and Mr. Parrot took a special train to West Palm Beach, then a boat from there to Ft. Lauderdale. Mr. McDonald, Mr. Flagler's contractor, accompanied them. Mrs. Tuttle met them at Ft. Lauderdale and brought them to Ft. Dallas in a wagon and a buckboard.

They arrived here late in the afternoon, looked the situation over, and before midnight of that night, on Mrs. Tuttle's front porch, an agreement was entered into with Mrs. Tuttle and Mrs. Brickell whereby Mr. Flagler was to build his railroad to Ft. Dallas, build a hotel, a freight and passenger depot, and was also to lay out the City of Miami. In return, Mrs. Tuttle and Mrs. Brickell were to give half of their holdings in real estate [within the city limits] *to Mr. Flagler. Mr. Flagler instructed Mr. McDonald to build the hotel, Mr. Parrot to extend the railroad to Miami, and Mr. Ingraham to lay out the city.*[220]

WILLIAM'S PROPHECY WAS TO BE REALIZED! And it was William who had set the entire chain of events in motion with people he had known in Cleveland that would now result in a railroad and the founding of two great American cities. He brought Ephraim Sturtevant from Cleveland to Biscayne Bay, where they discovered an isolated tropical paradise. Sturtevant and his wife, Frances, then moved there with the Brickells. Julia Sturtevant Tuttle visited her parents and moved from Cleveland to the mouth of the Miami River after her husband, Frederick Tuttle, died of tuberculosis. John D. Rockefeller introduced Julia to Henry Flagler, both men former residents of Cleveland.

Julia and the Brickells wanted to create a city at the mouth of the Miami River. The Brickells also wanted to carve out a town on their property at New River. Flagler owned a railroad and could be persuaded with gifts of land to push it south along the eastern Florida seaboard.

The "Magic City" and the "Venice of America" were to be created!

Chapter 9

Flagler's Railroad

IN 1926, A MIAMI HURRICANE FLOODED the basement of the Bulmer Apartments that were built and owned by William Brickell Jr., oldest son of William and Mary Brickell. Two trunks filled with Brickell family records, documents and photos were destroyed, "probably the most accurate accounting of Miami's founding days," lamented the *Miami News*.[221] On the other hand, Tuttle family records have survived the years, making it easier for historians to document Julia Tuttle's role in persuading Henry M. Flagler to bring a railroad to Miami.

Moreover, according to Thelma Peters, the Tuttle family has "always been involved in preserving South Florida history in their support of the historical association and museum,"[222] while "the Brickell family [has] stayed out of the limelight [and] no one of them ever seems to have anything to do with local history."[223]

From a comment in Maude Brickell's short 3¼-page biographical sketch of her parents, one might surmise that perhaps the Brickells kept their distance and were not easily accessible to local historians because they felt the family had not always been portrayed fairly. After a brief accounting of her parents' lives as she understood it, Maude breaks off abruptly with, "I could go on and on, but what's the use."[224]

For whatever reason history has treated them differently, there is no disputing that William and Mary were every bit as responsible as Julia for Flagler's decision to bring the railroad to Biscayne Bay that resulted in the founding of Miami and Fort Lauderdale.

IT IS CLEAR FROM EXISTING LETTERS WRITTEN by Flagler and his land commissioner, James Ingraham, that the Brickells were coordinating efforts with Julia in the mid-1890s to entice Flagler with proposals. Correspondence from Flagler to Julia, dated April 22, 1895, mentions a letter that he has "addressed to Mr. Brickell in reply to his offer sent me by Mr. Ingraham."[225]

Both Julia and the Brickells were offering Flagler half their property in what would be a city of Miami two miles long and one mile wide in exchange for extending his railroad from Palm Beach to Biscayne Bay, building a first-class hotel and laying out a town site. Julia's half of 640 acres excluded her 13-acre homesite and 23 acres retained by Joseph H. Day when he sold his interest in the tract to her.

The Brickells were not only offering half their land in what would become Miami but also were sweetening their offer with an additional one hundred acres at New River, twenty-six miles to the north of Miami, in exchange for Flagler building a depot for a future town to be called Fort Lauderdale.

The Brickells owned 3,974 acres of land on either side of New River stretching four miles west from the ocean beach. The Frankie Lewis Donation, one of the four land grants they had purchased from Harriet English in 1874, consisted of 640 acres, and on January 8, 1890, they had acquired another 3,334 acres from the Florida Land and Mortgage Company for $5,002[226] ($118,291 in 2008). A depot and stop on the railway line at New River would allow the Brickells to establish a town site on their property, greatly enhancing the value of all their land in the area.

Flagler mentions the Brickell offer in the letter of April 22, 1895, to Julia: "Included in Mr. Brickell's proposition was one hundred acres at New River... not that I expect to build up a town at New River, but I think it is good farming land and I should hope to recoup myself to some extent by the sale of property given me in that neighborhood."[227]

Flagler's reluctance "to build up a town at New River" is understandable, as not even a settlement existed there at the time. A very early settlement was decimated in 1836 by a Seminole attack known as the Cooley Massacre. In 1895, only six whites inhabited the area: Frank Stranahan, who operated a small Indian trading post, an overnight camp and a ferry on the north side of New River west of Tarpon Bend; Mr. and Mrs. A.J. Wallace, who worked for Stranahan; Dennis O'Neill, keeper of a house of refuge that had been established by the federal government on the ocean beach to accommodate survivors of shipwrecks; William C. Valentine, a surveyor who lived at Burnham's Point in the Harbor Beach area; and recent arrival, E.T. King, who homesteaded because he had heard a railroad was coming.[228]

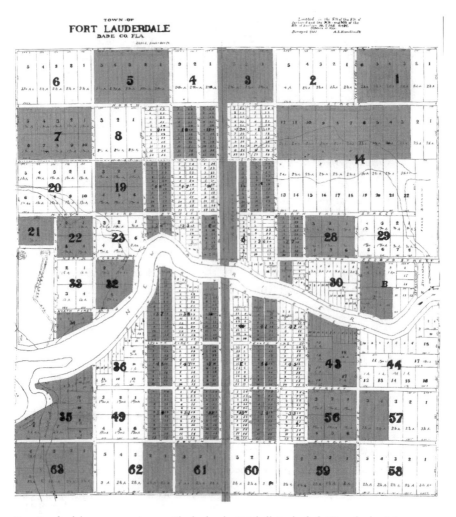

Fort Lauderdale property given to Flagler by the Brickells is shaded. City plat by A.L. Knowlton for William and Mary Brickell, dated April 20, 1896.

Although Flagler saw little benefit to himself in a town site at New River, the Brickells prevailed in their negotiations with him. He brought his railroad to where the Brickells platted and subdivided a one-square-mile city west of the Frankie Lewis Donation. Flagler built a station there, developed the town's streets and agreed to promote a city of Fort Lauderdale in his advertising and publicity.[229] In exchange, the Brickells gave him not 100 acres but half their land, approximately 248 acres in town lots (excluding river acreage), plus 21 acres for the railroad right of way.

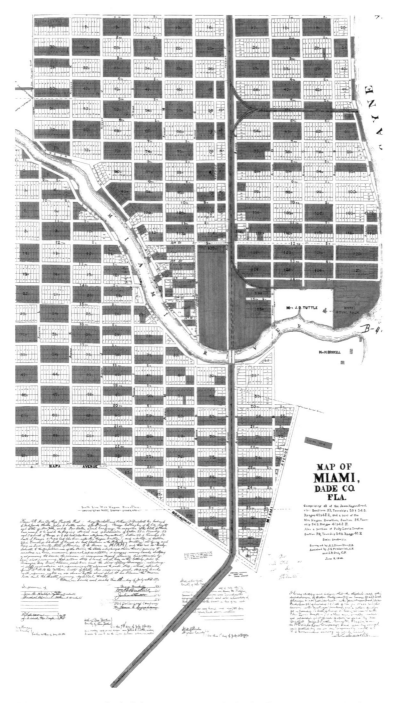

Miami property is shaded that was given to Flagler by the Brickells south of the river, and Tuttle north of the river. City plat by A.L. Knowlton for William and Mary Brickell, Julia Tuttle and Henry M. Flagler, dated June 9, 1896.

Street building kept pace with railroad construction, and the Florida East Coast Railway carried its first passengers into Fort Lauderdale on February 22, 1896.[230] The railroad reached Miami a month and a half later—the first train arriving on April 13 with Flagler on board.[231]

HISTORIANS HAVE CONSIDERED JULIA'S CONTRACT with Flagler of October 24, 1895, Miami's "birth certificate."[232] Yet the Brickells signed their contract with Flagler four and a half months earlier, on June 12, 1895.[233] Moreover, the Brickells were the first to deed land to Flagler. On August 29, 1895, they transferred to him a one-hundred-foot strip across their vast holdings in what are now Palm Beach and Broward Counties so that he could begin extending the railroad south from Palm Beach.[234] Julia didn't deed her first properties to Flagler until five months later on February 1, 1896, when she gave him one hundred acres around her homesite.[235]

Three months after this, on April 24 and May 1, the Brickells gave Flagler the bulk of the 269-acre gift in Fort Lauderdale.[236] On December 27, 1897, they gave him more lots in the new city with some swapping occurring between the parties on March 24 and April 30, 1898, that finalized the Fort Lauderdale conveyance.[237]

In the meantime, Miami was platted by the Brickells, Flagler and Julia after the Brickells gave Flagler 200 acres south of the river and Julia gave him 254 acres north of the river—both deeds dated January 6, 1897.[238]

Total acreage that each gave to Flagler was 469 from the Brickells and 354 from Julia, plus a one-hundred-foot right of way that each gave for the railroad on other properties between Palm Beach and Coconut Grove.

THE BRICKELLS MADE AN ADDITIONAL CONCESSION to make the deal happen with Flagler. There had been confusion for years about title to the one-hundred-acre tract north of the Miami River where the federal government had established Fort Dallas for its Seminole wars earlier in the century, where Julia had recently established her home site and where Flagler wanted to build his Royal Palm Hotel.

In spite of Julia's possession of the land as part of the 640 acres she purchased in 1890, the Brickells believed they owned the 100 acres because of a phrase in their original 1874 deed from Harriet English. The deed itemized four donations to be conveyed, followed by a blanket phrase giving "all other lots or parcels of land lying in the same township with the foregoing, viz the Miami Township."[239]

The one hundred acres north of the Miami River are in Township 54 South, the same township as the Rebecca Hagan (Egan) Donation, one of the land

Postcard depicting Flagler's Royal Palm Hotel in Miami, with Brickell Point across the bay in the background.

grants conveyed to the Brickells. Thus, the Brickells believed they had bought the one-hundred-acre tract. Originally, the one hundred acres were the John Egan Donation, and only later were they considered part of the James Hagan (Egan) Donation that Julia purchased.

Several years earlier, the Brickells had brought two lawsuits seeking to clear title to all of the land they purchased from English in 1874, including the one hundred acres north of the river. They received favorable decrees on May 13, 1888, and July 7, 1892, that cleared title to all of the land. (Actually, as land values skyrocketed, title challenges to Brickell land would persist and not finally be settled until the mid-twentieth century. Attorney/historian Patrick Scott meticulously documented many of the ensuing title challenges for his article, "The Many Heirs of Jonathan Lewis," published in the Summer/Fall 1994 issue of the *Broward Legacy*.)[240] Julia and Flagler insisted that Julia owned the one hundred acres. To settle the matter in the interest of getting the railroad, on January 15, 1896, the Brickells gave Julia a quitclaim deed to the acreage, relinquishing their claim to the tract.[241]

Maude indicates in her biographical sketch that her parents gave up their claim with some consternation: "A strange twist of fate gave Mr. Henry Flagler a deed to the property known then as Ft. Dallas. Mr. Brickell had a deed from Mrs. English, her brother Richard [Fitzpatrick], and a Spanish deed, a donation to John Eagan [*sic*]. The lawyers and judges said it was outlawed and it was gobbled up by Flagler."[242]

In fact, an 1869 deed filed in Richland County, South Carolina, a copy of which was obtained from the Key West–Dade County Recorder's Office, reveals that Harriet English sold 740 acres, consisting of the 100-acre John Egan Donation and the 640-acre James Hagan (Egan) Donation, to J.V. Harris, MD, a resident of Mississippi, on November 30, 1869. Thus, the 100-acre John Egan Donation was not in English's possession when the Brickells purchased the Rebecca Hagan (Egan) Donation and other land grants from her in 1874.[243]

In spite of whatever friction existed between the Brickells and Flagler from their earlier association in Cleveland due to a possible default on a loan and possible negative consequences to the Brickells as a result of the Rockefeller-Flagler "Cleveland Massacre," and whatever dispute may have existed between Julia and the Brickells over ownership of the John Egan Donation, the overriding goal for everybody was the railroad and creating a city on Brickell and Tuttle land.

Julia and the Brickells worked together to make this happen, but it was not without unexpected and unpleasant consequences for both.

Chapter 10

Debts and Betrayals

FOLLOWING CONSUMMATION OF THE DEAL with Flagler, Julia saw the coming of a railroad and creation of a city as an opportunity to add to her landholdings with the expectation that she would be able to sell her Miami lots and added acreage quickly and at a nice profit. But sales didn't happen quickly, and because her resources were limited, she was unable to cover short-term loans with high interest rates that she acquired from a variety of banks.

She turned to Flagler for help, asking him to "endorse" her notes. Assuming at first that her loans were to pay for work being done for his company, Flagler agreed to take responsibility for them. But soon it was apparent that Julia was borrowing from banks to add to her landholdings and to improve her existing properties. Although Flagler urged her to "not go in debt another dollar, no matter what the inducement may be,"[244] she continued borrowing. Even after the railroad reached Miami and the Royal Palm Hotel opened, Julia continued to go further into debt and ask Flagler for help.

When her obligations increased to $30,000 ($766,470 in 2008), an exasperated Flagler wrote: "I am very much worried over the financial situation... I hope that you will sell the Cleveland property and get yourself out of debt."[245]

Two weeks later, after receiving another bank note from her, he wrote: "If I endorse this note, it makes me responsible for $43,000 [$1,098,607 in 2008] of your indebtedness. With the understanding that this amount is not to be increased, I endorse the note."[246]

But it wasn't the end. With the next request, he wrote: "I cannot and must not increase my responsibility and you should not ask me to...I do

Illustration depicting the arrival of the first train to Miami on April 13, 1896.

not want you 'to suffer,' but I cannot accept the responsibility of your suffering. For months past I have advised against your becoming so deeply involved in debt."[247]

Finally, Julia's debt to Flagler amounted to $88,101 ($2,250,892 in 2008). James Ingraham, by now a vice-president of Flagler's operations, took charge of the out-of-control situation, and on December 27, 1897, Julia deeded to Flagler the value of $86,047 ($2,198,414 in 2008) in additional Miami lots, reducing her indebtedness to him to $2,054 ($52,478 in 2008).[248]

IN THE MEANTIME, TENSION HAD BUILT between the Brickells and Flagler as the railroad tracks inched from Palm Beach to Miami. The Royal Palm Hotel was under construction, and newly arrived entrepreneurs were establishing businesses on the north side of the river as fast as a tent could be put up and a frame store built.

A letter of February 24, 1896, from W.S. Graham, an attorney handling Flagler's interests in Miami, to J.R. Parrott, one of Flagler's vice-presidents, warned of "trouble ahead unless a change of policy occurs in Miami."[249] He explained:

> *The south side is not receiving the proper attention and the Brickells are getting very sore. They fear if everything is not ready at once on*

both sides of the river and the lots on both sides of the river put on the market simultaneously, that sales will get started on the north side first, and their opportunities of sale will be badly prejudiced... They feel that work on the streets on the south side should be pushed with equal vigor and that the promised bridge across the river should be under construction now and completed by the time the lots are placed on sale...In other words, they expect "a fair show."[250]

Graham's letter indicates that Flagler was supposed to build a bridge over the river and improve streets on the south side. An article in the *Miami Metropolis* of October 9, 1896, confirms that the terms of the contract and Flagler's obligations to the Brickells were for "the construction of a bridge across the river to connect their property with the north side. Mr. Flagler was also to pay for the survey and clearing of streets, all of his part to be performed on or before December 12th next [1896], or eighteen months after the date on which the contract was executed [June 12, 1895]."[251]

A year earlier, on December 10, 1895, Mary had posted a bond with the Dade County Commission to operate a ferry across the river.[252] But a ferry presented delays and fees that were inconvenient for people. If the south side was to be developed, a bridge would be absolutely necessary.

When Flagler finally completed a bridge in December 1896, it was a crude wooden structure located at what is now SW 2nd Avenue, far from where the Brickells wanted it built at Miami Avenue near their trading post and the logical commercial street for development on the south side.

One settler described the bridge: "There was only a narrow bridge across the Miami River, just wide enough for one wagon to cross at a time. And beyond the bridge the road had not yet been paved with crushed rock as it was to be later."[253]

Isidor Cohen, a merchant who established a clothing store on the south side but soon moved it across the river because of the difficulty his customers had crossing the river, referred to the bridge as "improvised."[254]

Harry Kersey summarized the cause of William's "very sore" feelings:

Isolated on the south bank of the river without a bridge connecting them to the activity on the other side, the Brickells soon lost their dominant place in the commercial life of the area. When a bridge was built, it went well to the west of Brickell Point, and this completed Brickell's alienation from Henry M. Flagler. He had not liked Flagler's imperious manner when he first came to negotiate

Photograph of Brickell Point with marl on bank, circa 1898.

> *for land, prior to extending his tracks into the Miami area; then, to make matters worse, the Flagler dredges had deposited a spoil bank in front of his home, obstructing the view. The old man reportedly vowed never to cross the river again.*[255]

Ralph Munroe elaborated on the spoil bank:

> *In dredging the river-mouth for its steamers, the new administration left a crescent-shaped pile of broken shell and marl thirty feet high on Brickell's Point, neatly encircling his house and cutting off all view of the river and bay! Brickell insisted that this was to have been distributed to fill in some low land, but there it lay until he found a means of getting something back by selling it for road-making material.*[256]

The next time Flagler sent for him, an angry William responded, "Tell Flagler he knows where to find me. Same distance from my place to his."[257]

William didn't cross the river for fifteen months until he had to go to court to successfully defend ownership of the Punch Bowl property. When he did cross the river, it was an occasion for an announcement in the *Miami Metropolis*: "Wm. B. Brickell, Sr. was in the city a couple of days this week attending the hearing in the case of Brickell vs. the Baron heirs. This is the first time Mr. Brickell has been on this side of the river since before the advent of the railroad."[258]

William seated on the porch of Brickell mansion in 1906 with his three sons on the steps: William II, Charles and George. The men standing are unidentified.

A diary entry from Emma Gilpin, a visitor to Miami in 1899 who knew the Brickells from an earlier trip in 1890, comments on William's feelings of betrayal by Flagler:

> [Mr. Brickell] *does not talk quite so much. He seems to have been rather overwhelmed by the power of Mr. Flagler to whom he says he has given 200 acres of land...The Miami River has been dredged*

and the white rock has been heaped upon his shore, which looks distressing...He seems to be quite satisfied that he has reaped no benefit from Flagler. Says he is going to sell out to a syndicate and go to Australia. Thinks in this country a man is smart when he can get ahead of his neighbor. Thinks there is not much Christianity here. He hoped to have Flagler build his town south of the Miami River on his land and has been much disappointed...[259]

Flagler apparently complied just enough with the terms of his contract with the Brickells to avoid a lawsuit.

William, a "teetotaler" according to Maude, was also "bitter" because liquor was sold to Indians and others north of the river, and then, inebriated, they would sometimes come south of the river and cause "trouble."[260]

William didn't "sell out to a syndicate and go to Australia," but he and Mary did make at least two more trips to Australia in these years to visit Mary's family members. In 1900, they traveled in a first-class cabin on the *Mariposa* from San Francisco to Sydney, arriving September 30, 1900.[261] A source states that they stayed in Australia for five months on this trip.[262] Four years later, they left London on the RMS *India* in a first-class cabin, arriving at Sydney on January 8, 1904.[263]

ALTHOUGH ARGUABLY THE BRICKELL PROPERTY on the south side offered the best building sites, the town of Miami was built on the north side. Mary, who obtained one of the first six real estate licenses issued by the young city, initially hoped to sell commercial lots on the south. She advertised business lots for $300 in the first issue of the *Miami Metropolis*, May 15, 1896. But with only rocky dirt trails on the south and an "improvised" bridge at an inconvenient location, she had to change her intentions.

Neither William nor Julia lived to see the exorbitant profits their land would bring. Ralph Munroe commented on the disappointments of both:

The early growth of the town was not what Mrs. Tuttle expected. In fact, in the first years it was largely a fiat development in which Flagler continued to build ahead of actual demand to stimulate interest and get things started. The result was bitter disappointment for Mrs. Tuttle whose land remained vacant, weed-grown and in little demand until her death. In later years, of course, it became immensely valuable to her heirs...Though [William Brickell] lived to see his lands of far greater value than he had ever hoped for, he, too, died before their development into the best part of Miami and the growth of prices that even he could scarcely have believed.[264]

Julia died suddenly at age forty-nine on September 13, 1898, after recurring migraine headaches, only two and a half years after the arrival of the railroad.

Although William Brickell lived to see the railroad brought to Miami that he had prophesied about in the 1870s to "incredulous smiles" and saw his "visionary" investment in South Florida vindicated, he died a bitter man at age eighty-three on January 14, 1908, following a stroke.

In his later years, some referred to William as "old man Brickell" and thought of him as a "crank." But Munroe expressed a different opinion: "In defense of William Brickell, it must be stated that he was a pragmatic visionary, a man who could see magnificent possibilities where few thought to even look. To the cynic and naysayer he responded, 'Yes I can.' He was also a man of backbone, grit, and determination, all traits that were the hallmark of a true pioneer."[265]

Although William became "overwhelmed" by Flagler, Mary Brickell did not let the railroad baron dampen her spirits. In Thelma Peters's words, Mary "was taking over the finances and doing it with integrity and wisdom."[266] She would go on to triumph in ways that even the "visionary" William could never have imagined.

Chapter 11

Mary's Extraordinary
Legacy

S HORTLY BEFORE SHE PASSED AWAY on January 13, 1922, Mary Brickell wrote an open letter to Miamians that was published in the *Miami Herald*. In it she said, "Everything I have done in the past has been with the idea of helping Miami."[267] Indeed, she did more than any other individual to help the young city.

Oh, but you say, what about Julia Tuttle, who has been designated the "Mother of Miami"?[268] Mary gave more land than Julia to entice Henry Flagler to bring a railroad to Biscayne Bay, signed a contract to do so four and a half months before Julia signed "the birth certificate of Miami"[269] and began deeding land to Flagler five months before Julia. Moreover, while Julia lived in Miami and gave to the young city for seven years, Mary gave to the city and its citizens for fifty-one years.

The Brickells arrived at what would become Miami twenty years before Julia, when the area was a wilderness populated by distrustful Seminoles who had massacred settlers as recently as thirteen years prior to their arrival. By offering the Indians friendship and giving them a way to interact economically with whites, buying for cash what they had to sell and treating them fairly, Mary and William pacified the Seminoles.

Apart from the Brickells building trust with the Seminoles to the benefit of all the settlers, and the large role they played in bringing a railroad to Miami, they did far more to help South Florida—especially Mary, who lived another fourteen years after William's death in 1908.

THE BRICKELLS OWNED THREE MILES OF the finest frontage on Biscayne Bay, a spectacular hammock with rocky cliffs south of the Miami River. Since business was established north of the river after the advent of the railroad, "southside" became primarily residential. Mary put the initial Brickell lots on the market the same week the *Metropolis* began publishing the city's newspaper on May 15, 1896. The *Metropolis* reported:

> *The sale of the Brickell lots on the south side of the river began last Monday. The first sale was made to Kirk Munroe, the well-known novelist, who happened to be in the* Metropolis *office when the map of the Brickell lots was first unrolled to the public eye. He bought two fine lots...*[that] *are among the best in town and cost only $300* [$7,665 in 2008] *for the corner and $250* [$6,387 in 2008] *for the adjoining lot.*[270]

Mary put their property on the market incrementally and gradually. Some complained that the Brickells were holding back the growth of the city by not making all of their property available early on and at affordable prices. Settlers especially wanted to buy homesites overlooking Biscayne Bay. But Mary

Brickell Avenue in 2009.

believed that Miami would be better served if the superb bay front was saved for quality homes and apartments when the city's growth could support them.

Dr. Joe Knetsch has studied early 1890s correspondence from Brickell critics to officials in Tallahassee and Washington. He found that "much of this criticism came from rival land dealers and others who wanted to develop the land for their own personal benefit...With the Brickells holding so much prime land on the bay, they were a natural target for some rather unscrupulous letter-writers."[271]

As the city's population grew, Mary opened up more sections of the family's landholdings. In 1911, she platted and paved Miami's most glamorous boulevard, Brickell Avenue, stretching from the Miami River south to Coconut Grove, and had trees, shrubbery and flowers planted along the median in keeping with her vision of making Miami "the garden spot of the world."[272] Then she gave the thoroughfare to the city with a gift deed on March 6, 1913.[273]

Agnes Ash would later write in the *Miami News*:

> *Mrs. Brickell wanted a boulevard through her property after the railroad came and business promised to grow to fantastic heights. She didn't bother the politicians about it. Instead she ordered the concrete and other supplies from Germany, put her boy Will in charge of a road-building gang, and ordered a street 100 feet wide with parkways for planting shrubbery and flowers down the center.*[274]

Wide streets were one of Mary's cardinal principles. She had been disappointed that Henry Flagler didn't give the city wider streets on the north side of the river. "Time after time, in the early days of Miami," she said, "I endeavored to impress upon Mr. Flagler the necessity of widening the narrow streets of Miami."[275]

Mary also wanted Miami to be "a city of handsome homes."[276] She sold large bay-front tracts to people of national prominence who built mansions overlooking the bay, people such as Louis Comfort Tiffany, of stained-glass window and lamp fame, and William Jennings Bryan, the Democratic nominee for president in 1896, 1900 and 1908 and secretary of state under President Woodrow Wilson.

On January 5, 1914, Mary sold 180 acres at the south end of "Millionaire's Row," as Brickell Avenue became known, to James Deering, vice-president of International Harvester.[277] There Deering built Villa Vizcaya, a stunning thirty-four-room Italian Renaissance mansion filled with treasures collected

Villa Vizcaya.

from all over the world and with expansive Italian gardens and fountains on the grounds. Miami had a population of ten thousand at the time, and one thousand of its citizens were employed as laborers and craftsmen building the Vizcaya estate, completed in 1916.

A PERSONAL GLIMPSE OF MARY BRICKELL was given in an interview by a young woman, Ethel Weatherly Sherman, who was a stenographer with the law firm of Seymour & Atkinson:

> *When Mr. Seymour had papers for Mrs. Brickell or some of the family to sign, they would send me over there with them. As I think of Mrs. Brickell, she looked to me more like some pictures that you see of Queen Victoria. She was English and a very nice person...If there* [were] *any of them in the room she would introduce me to them, so I met a good many of them...* [Their house] *was like pictures that you see of the old Victorian houses full of bric-a-brac and beautiful old furniture...She was always nice to me. They always had crackers and cookies and tea, so I had quite a little visit there while I was waiting for her to read and sign the papers.*[278]

It was most unusual in the late nineteenth and early twentieth centuries for a woman to be as involved with business affairs as Mary was, and some men resented her for it. One man referred to her as "steely eyed."[279] Another called her "vile" and thought William wasn't much of a man for allowing Mary to handle the family's vast business interests.[280]

But more enlightened men held Mary in high regard. After her death at age eighty-six, the *Miami Herald* wrote:

> *The first comers to the city of Miami are today unanimous in praising the quick, keen mind behind the bright blue eyes of this woman pioneer whom they characterized as "one of the finest business women in the whole country." They speak almost reverently of her ability in managing the immense business which grew about as a result of her land holdings...*
>
> *Only the day before her death, Mrs. Brickell received several real estate men in Miami. Her keenness, the quickness and alertness of her mind, as well as the charm of her personality, made a deep impression upon them. "She will stand in my mind as one of the most delightful and one of the most uniquely interesting people I have ever met," said one of them.*[281]

The meeting the day before Mary's death was related to a new subdivision that she designed, platted and developed at her own expense. She called the subdivision Brickell Hammock, but its popular name became "The Roads." The five-hundred-acre neighborhood, stretching from 15th to 32nd Road between SW 1st Avenue and SW 11th Street, still reflects her taste and vision today. The area features her signature wide streets with median parkways and roundabouts graced with native trees, shrubbery and flowers. She envisioned residents walking the sidewalks and enjoying the beauty of their neighborhood.

Mary gave the streets, parkways and sidewalks of The Roads to the city, along with electric lights up and down each street. A developer working with Mary was quoted: "The streets and avenues in this subdivision will all be white ways. Mrs. Brickell is donating to the city of Miami a cool $100,000 [$1,273,943 in 2008] worth of improvements in this item alone. The city has been asked for nothing."[282]

The Roads was intended to provide affordable lots to Miami residents. All of the properties were sold at a one-day auction on February 1, 1923. The *Miami Herald* reported, "Over $300,000 [$3,821,828 in 2008] was realized from the sale, the average price being about $1,800 [$22,931 in 2008]."[283]

Mary developed other affordable subdivisions in Miami, such as Riverside between today's SW 7th and 8th Avenues.[284] She expanded the area in 1919 and personally financed many modest but comfortable homes there for residents.[285]

She also developed subdivisions in Fort Lauderdale to encourage the growth of that city. Two large subdivisions, Colee Hammock and Rio Vista,

The Roads auction in 1923.

were platted in 1920 on the one-square-mile Frankie Lewis Donation adjacent to and west of the Fort Lauderdale township platted earlier by the Brickells.[286] (In 1924, Rio Vista was deeded to C.J. Hector and was then re-platted.)[287] As with all of Mary's subdivisions, the roads, thoroughfares and utilities were dedicated to the perpetual use of the public.

Mary gave the citizens of Fort Lauderdale another gift that wasn't intended. The public gained riparian rights on either side of the river that cut through the middle of Fort Lauderdale when Mary lost a lawsuit brought against her by the city. Although she sold to private parties river frontage that was to include land "abutting and adjoining the river," the Florida Supreme Court agreed with a lower court on appeal that the original plat by the Brickells did not clearly reserve to themselves the riverbanks alongside North and South Streets that bordered the river, and, therefore, "dedication of the streets extends to the waters of New River."[288]

IN MIAMI, APART FROM DEVELOPING BEAUTIFUL residential neighborhoods at different price levels, Mary tried helping the young city in other ways. In the early years, Miami depended almost exclusively on income from wealthy vacationers who came during winter months and then disappeared until the following year. Mary was farsighted enough to realize that in order for Miami to achieve its potential as a major city, it needed industries other than tourism.

Brickell Point in 2009.

In 1898, she and William gave the city six acres between Brickell Avenue and Biscayne Bay to be used by the U.S. Department of Agriculture for an "Experimental Station" to develop "exotic plants and shrubbery."[289] Dr. David Fairchild, famed botanist and plant explorer, was instrumental in establishing a plant introduction site on the property that was in use until the facility was moved to southern Dade County in 1921.[290]

In 1903, the Brickells tried to help the city attract cigar factories. An early merchant, Isidor Cohen, recalled their effort:

> *The Brickell family...conveyed 200 building lots and a square block of land situated in its center to the Miami Board of Trade...for the exclusive purpose of securing cigar factories for Miami, the square block of land to be reserved for the erection of factory buildings, and after a certain term of years their sites to be conveyed to the factory owners. The purchasers of the lots were to erect dwellings for the [workers] of the proposed factories.*
>
> *Unfortunately, the scheme proved abortive because of lack of adequate transportation facilities and the difficulty apprehended*

by manufacturers in keeping Cuban labor in as small a town as Miami was then.[291]

These gifts to the city were with the stipulation that the property would revert back to the Brickell family when and if their intended purpose was unfulfilled.

With the same stipulation, Mary gave to the city a two-and-a-half-acre park in the 500 block of Brickell Avenue next to the family homesite.[292] The park is maintained by the city today and provides the public with access to Biscayne Bay from Brickell Avenue. In the park is an empty Brickell family mausoleum. Maude, who was the last to live in the family home until her death on November 22, 1960, had the family's remains removed to Woodlawn Cemetery on August 30, 1951. She said that Brickell Avenue had become "too noisy even for the dead."[293]

The city's first cemetery also was a Brickell property. William and Mary sold a ten-acre tract to the city for a Miami City Cemetery on June 24, 1897, for a nominal $750.[294]

Brickell Park with empty Brickell family mausoleum.

MARY BRICKELL GAVE GENEROUSLY NOT ONLY TO the city but to its citizens as well. A contemporary said, "Mary Brickell didn't believe in using banks and always had plenty of cash, which she loaned without collateral to people who were refused bank loans. Her interest-free loans helped many people open businesses."[295]

Upon Mary's death, the *Miami Herald* noted: "First comers to the city... remember with enthusiasm her approachability in the matter of loans and mortgages, without which, they say, early Miami would have had a far slower development."[296]

During the Panic of 1907, when banks failed and those that didn't were reluctant to make loans and provide mortgages, it was said that Edith, one of the Brickell daughters, went around with a large satchel-like purse lending money without collateral or interest to those in need.[297]

Blacks lined up in front of the Brickell home on Sundays to pay back money Mary had loaned them. She was kind to blacks, even, on occasion, utilizing her early skills as a dressmaker in Australia to make clothes for their children.[298]

The day after she died, seven leaders of the black community put a notice in the newspaper to express their gratitude for Mary's generosity to their community:

> *The death of Mrs. Mary Brickell...is a distinct loss to this section of Florida and particularly to the colored people of Miami, whom she helped in every practicable way to become not only property holders, but better citizens. Her general query to them was not so much "What have you?" but, "How are you living?"...The colored people of Miami, along with others, will feel her loss keenly.*[299]

Although many whites and blacks were never able to return the money she had lent them, Mary never foreclosed on a mortgage or took legal action to collect a loan.[300]

After she passed away in 1922, an accounting of her estate revealed that she was holding unpaid loans in the amount of $49,827 ($634,767 in 2008) and outstanding mortgages totaling $781,734 ($9,958,842 in 2008).[301]

The executors of her will estimated the value of her estate at $5 to $6 million ($64 to $76 million in 2008).[302] But a court case—not concerned with paying taxes on the estate!—estimated the worth of her property in just one of her land grants, the Polly Lewis Donation, at $12 million (just under $153 million in 2008).[303]

WILLIAM AND MARY BRICKELL WERE RESPECTED by the early leaders of Miami for their significant contributions to the young city.

One month after the railroad arrived and the *Metropolis* began publishing the city's first newspaper, Walter S. Graham, the editor, honored Julia Tuttle and the Brickells with gifts of the second and third newspapers off the press, reserving the first for the *Metropolis*.[304]

When the first aldermen were selected after the new city was incorporated on July 28, 1896, Julia and the Brickells were each asked whom they wanted to represent them as aldermen, and their choices were honored.

Ralph Munroe summed up the Brickells: "One may remark [on] the evidence of sound character and judgment in the Brickells in that neither the labors and hardships of wilderness poverty nor the sudden flood of riches which followed could disturb their industrious, cheerful, well-ordered lives."[305]

Six Brickell children survived their mother—Alice, Will, Charles, Belle, Maude and George. It was a tightknit family, with each of the members contributing his or her talents to achieve family goals. At the time of their

Brickell mansion in 1906 with William seated on the porch; his three sons, William II, Charles and George, on the steps; and Belle and Maude on the balcony. The men standing are unidentified.

mother's death, all six adult children were residing in the twenty-two-room Brickell mansion. The daughters never married. The three sons were sent away to private schools, colleges and universities for an education and did marry, though none of their descendants survives today. The last of the direct line was William Barnwell Brickell IV, known as Butch, a Hollywood stuntman who died at age forty-six on October 13, 2003.[306]

Brickell family members never promoted William and Mary's contributions to Miami. And because family documents and photos were lost in a hurricane flood in the early twentieth century, the importance of the Brickells has been largely overlooked by historians and journalists who have given full credit for the founding of Miami to Julia Tuttle and Henry Flagler.

In the 1960s, one Miami citizen became disturbed enough about the historical injustice to William and Mary Brickell to make it the purpose of her life for the next forty years to try to right the wrong.

Chapter 12

The Mary Brickell Lady

CARMEN PETSOULES, A FEISTY CUBAN AMERICAN, is fondly known as the "Mary Brickell Lady" for her passionate promotion of William and Mary Brickell, especially Mary. Some have wondered how "this little Cuban," as she refers to herself, became interested in Mary.[307]

Carmen Mirta Vidal was born in Havana on June 17, 1926. After graduating from high school, she became a secretary to an attorney in Havana. She began visiting Miami on holidays and, on one of her visits, met and fell in love with a Greek American, James Emmanuel Petsoules, who owned a Greek restaurant on Miami Avenue in what is now Mary Brickell Village.

After marrying Petsoules, Carmen moved to Miami and became a U.S. citizen. In 1968, the couple bought a home on SW 25th Road in The Roads, the quiet neighborhood located today between Little Havana and Coconut Grove.

The first afternoon of living in The Roads, Carmen met her across-the-street neighbor, Rosabelle Peacock, an elderly lady who was from a pioneer Miami family. Mrs. Peacock's father, Simon Frow, had been the keeper of the lighthouse at Cape Florida, and she was the widow of Charles Peacock, who was from another pioneer family.

In her first visit with Mrs. Peacock, Carmen made a comment about the beauty of The Roads, especially the broad boulevards with parks along the medians graced with trees, shrubbery and colorful flowers. Mrs. Peacock replied: "Mary Brickell designed all this and gave the parkways to the city. She was a pioneer and this was her land. She gave so much to Miami, but local historians have credited someone else with all that she did."

Rosabelle Peacock.

Carmen continued, "This sparked my interest in Mary and in the fact that she had not been recognized for her contributions to the city."

Carmen began visiting almost daily with Mrs. Peacock, who told her about the pioneer days of Miami and especially about the Brickells. Mrs. Peacock's mother had been friendly with Mary Brickell.

"I began taking notes," Carmen says, "and I became passionately interested in Mary. I started going to local libraries searching for clippings and anything I could find about the Brickells. There was not very much in the records about Mary. The negative impression that had been given by local historians was that she was reclusive, unfriendly and cantankerous."

No known photo existed of Mary, and finding one became a particular goal. Over the years, Carmen made periodic searches of photographs and clippings about the Brickell family at the Historical Museum of Southern Florida. Photos existed of the Brickell children and a couple of William but none of Mary. Then, in 1992, Carmen came across a snapshot of Maude, the youngest daughter of William and Mary, standing outside the Brickell home with an elderly woman.

"I knew the young woman in the photo was Maude because she was wearing the same hat I had seen her wear in other photos," Carmen explained. "I wondered who the elderly lady was with her. I happened to turn over the photo and on the back was written, 'Mother and myself.' I realized that I had found the first known photo of Mary Brickell. I screamed at the top of my

Carmen Petsoules holding up the "Mother and myself" snapshot.

lungs, 'Bingo! I found Mary!' The museum staff came running to find out what I was screaming about."

The snapshot had been donated to the museum three years prior to that time but had not been recognized for its historical value. Since then, other photos of both Mary and William have been donated to the museum.

IN 1984, CARMEN EXPANDED HER INTEREST from collecting clippings about the Brickells to becoming an activist on their behalf. The Department of Transportation had notified residents of The Roads that it intended to eliminate the parkway on SW 25th Road and make the street a continuation of I-95.

"I was immediately upset," Carmen exclaimed. "They're going to take away Mary's beautiful parkway! Then we learned that the DOT planned to destroy by eminent domain all the houses from 25th to 32nd Road between SW 1st and 2nd Avenue to create a parking lot for the Vizcaya Metrorail Station. Rosabelle encouraged me to fight it."

Carmen spearheaded a meeting of residents from The Roads, and they formed the Miami Roads Neighborhood Civic Association.

She continued,

Some fifty to one hundred of our people attended a City Commission public hearing. They weren't expecting us. One commissioner, Willie Gort, said, "This is the first time I've seen people from The Roads get together for anything."

One of our members, Armando Framil, got up and told the commissioners that we didn't want what DOT had proposed. Others went to the microphone. I made a big issue about the historical value of Mary's design for The Roads. Finally after our continuing protests the commissioners agreed with us.

Then the DOT came up with a new idea. They wanted to remove the banyan trees and Mary's parkway in the middle of Coral Way to widen the street. This street, Southwest Third Avenue, was the one commercial street Mary planned for The Roads.

We went to the library for hours and hours looking for clippings from newspapers to show that Mary had platted the area. Rosabelle told us where to research. A few attorneys were in our group. We found Mary's will in an abstract for my house. In it was information about The Roads deed.

Joe Wilkins, on our board, spoke at a public hearing before the commission and pointed out that Mary had platted The Roads, which included Coral Way. He said they had to respect what she had done. The city attorney checked what we were talking about and agreed. His confirmation convinced the commission of our position, and Coral Way was preserved as Mary had intended.

THESE SUCCESSES MOTIVATED CARMEN TO TAKE steps to make Miamians more aware of the Brickells. She learned of items that had been given by Maude Brickell to Stan Cooper, an amateur historian in Miami, and other items that Cooper had rescued from the Brickell mansion after Maude passed away and the house was being torn down in 1961.

Carmen gained permission to exhibit Cooper's collection, as well as Brickell items in the possession of Carol Snyder of Ocala, granddaughter of Mrs. DeMarise Purdy, companion and housekeeper of Maude Brickell. Three annual May 1 exhibits were held from 1991 to 1993 at Simpson Park, located in The Roads, and the public was invited to attend free of charge.

Prior to the second exhibit in 1992, Carmen knocked on the door of Marjorie Brickell, widow of William and Mary's grandson, William Barnwell

Brickell III. Mrs. Brickell lived in Coral Gables with her son, William Barnwell Brickell IV, known as Butch. Mrs. Brickell was out playing tennis, but Carmen spoke to Butch and left a note for his mother inviting her to the exhibit.

Marjorie Brickell came to the exhibit and met Carmen, and afterward they became friendly. Having contact with members of the Brickell family spurred Carmen to greater activism.

The State of Florida planned a new $15.5 million Brickell Avenue bridge connecting downtown Miami north of the river with the financial district south of the river. The bridge would celebrate the 100th birthday of Miami in 1996 by linking its future with its past. It was to feature a sculpture by Miami artist Manuel Carbonell depicting a Tequesta warrior, mother and child and bas-reliefs commemorating famous people in Miami's history— Julia Tuttle, Henry Flagler, Everglades grande dame Marjory Stoneman Douglas and William Brickell. But not Mary!

"I learned that Mary was not to be included in the bas-reliefs," Carmen said. "I was told by the Downtown Development Authority that it had been an oversight but not to say anything because it would delay the opening and dedication of the bridge. I went to Manuel, and he agreed with me that Mary should be included."

Carbonell designed a large bas-relief for the base of the

Brickell Avenue bridge bas-relief of Mary, William and Tequesta Indians.

bridge that depicts Mary, William and the Tequesta, an early Native American tribe that resided in the Miami area. The bas-relief faces a circular pattern thirty-eight feet in diameter of postholes cut in bedrock that was discovered in 1998 where William Brickell's warehouse once stood. The pattern, now called the "Miami Circle," is attributed to the Tequesta and was declared a National Historic Landmark in 2009. It is thought that the circular pattern "represents the footprint of a prehistoric structure, probably constructed of wood and thatch...[that was] either a council house or chief's house."[308]

Carmen continued, "Marge and Butch became active with me for certain other goals. In 1921, Mary had given the city a 2½-acre bay-front property adjacent to the Brickell mansion for a public park. On it was the Brickell mausoleum. In 1988, the city wanted to put a high-rise there. Then a developer wanted to buy Brickell Point and they were supposed to move the mausoleum there."

Carmen and the Brickells objected to the idea. Carmen found Mary's original gift deed showing that the land given to the city is to be "set apart, preserved and maintained as a private burial ground for my family" and is "dedicated" for that purpose.[309]

"Marge and Butch threatened to take back the land," Carmen continued. "The judge said, 'If the city doesn't want the park it gets returned to the Brickell family.'" The park and mausoleum stayed where Mary intended.

Preserving Mary Brickell's intentions has led Carmen to successfully protest other threats to Mary's vision for Miami, such as eliminating the Brickell Avenue parkway and narrowing various parkways in The Roads. Carmen explained, "Mary wanted Miami to be beautiful. She designed Brickell Avenue as a wide boulevard with a park along the median and similar landscaped medians and roundabouts throughout The Roads. She had them constructed at her own expense and gave them to the city. I wanted to do something to make it impossible to eliminate Mary's parkways."

Earlier, Carmen had formed the Mary Brickell Garden Club. The group had planted trees in Mary's honor. Carmen presented a new idea to the Garden Club, the Roads Association and the Pioneers' Club—a group of Miami pioneer families that had made Carmen a member as a civic activist. The idea was to raise $18,000 to establish a monument to Mary on Brickell Avenue.

The money was raised by selling $25 bricks and $100 foundation tiles imprinted with names of the donors. At the top of the base was a bust of Mary Brickell sculpted by West Palm Beach artist Beto Alvarez. In 1998, the City Commission and Mayor Joe Carrillo passed a resolution to erect the monument on the Brickell Avenue median between SE 6th and 7th Streets.

Right: Carmen with Butch Brickell at the commemoration of the monument to Mary.

Below: The Roads commemoration plaque.

In an effort to protect the parkways of The Roads, in 2006 Carmen successfully lobbied the City Commission to place a plaque in the median at 25th Road and SW 2nd Avenue. The plaque commemorates the spot where Mary dedicated the subdivision three days before she passed away at age eighty-six on January 13, 1922.

Carmen explained, "Mary personally supervised plans and specifications for The Roads, which she called 'Brickell Hammock.'"

The plaque, located cater-corner from Carmen's house, was to be dedicated on December 27, 2006. The day before the ceremony, she happened to be standing on her porch when a City of Miami Solid Waste Department truck stopped in front of her house, extended a bucket, scooped the plaque out of the ground and dumped it in with the rest of the day's garbage. The plaque had been wrapped in plastic awaiting the dedication.

"Right away I started screaming," Carmen exclaimed. "I ran over to a city employee standing nearby as the truck drove away." After phone calls to the waste department and City Commissioner Joe Sanchez, the undamaged plaque was returned.

Other efforts by Carmen have resulted in SW 25th Road being named "Mary Brickell Road," SW 26th Road named "Pioneer Road" and SE 6th Street between Brickell Avenue and Miami Avenue designated "Butch Brickell Way."

Carmen has been honored for her civic activism on behalf of the Brickells. Mayor Stephen B. Clark issued a proclamation declaring December 8, 1995, "Carmen Petsoules Day" because of her "commitment to the preservation of Miami's history for future generations." The proclamation commended her as "the epitome of the achiever who through dedication and hard work knows how to reach her goals. Ms. Petsoules' work as a historian led to the designation of Brickell Hammock Parkways, Mary Brickell Road and Mary on the Bridge."[310]

In 1998, the Dade Heritage Trust, Miami's largest historic preservation organization, bestowed on Carmen the Henriette Harris Award, the trust's highest honor, "for your extraordinary efforts to preserve Miami's heritage by honoring the memory of Mary Brickell."[311]

And the eighty-four-year-old Carmen isn't finished! "I hope to get the help of the mayor to place The Roads on the National Register of Historic Places so that Mary's beautiful design for the neighborhood can never be altered," she said. "This will be my last hurrah," she continued. "After your dad, Marge and Butch passed away, I lost all of my support. I just hope that others after me will take up the banner for Mary and William. They are the true founders of Miami, and someone will be able to prove it."

Notes

Introduction

1. Letter from Thelma Peters to Carter Brickell, September 27, 1985.
2. Letter from Thelma Peters to Carter Brickell, November 24, 1985.
3. The Inflation Calculator, westegg.com/inflation/infl/cgi.
4. Catherine Merriman was born on June 17, 1811, to William and Mary Moore Merriman in Castle Donnington, Leicester, England. Retrieved from British Ancestors April 3, 2005, for Carmen Petsoules.
5. Joseph Bulmer and Catherine Merryman [*sic*], marriage records, Lancashire, England, film 0438196. Retrieved by Ancestor Seekers, Salt Lake City, Utah, for Carmen Petsoules, March 31, 2005.
6. Kleinberg, "Newfound Pictures."
7. Maude Brickell, "Maude Brickell Manuscript," transcribed by Margot Ammidown in 1981 from handwritten biographical sketch thought to have been dictated by Maude to her housekeeper, Mrs. DeMarise Purdy, Historical Museum of Southern Florida, 2.
8. Kleinberg, "Newfound Pictures."
9. Ibid.

Chapter 1

10. *Biographical Review*, "David Z. Brickell," 334. Retrieved May 26, 2009, from Historic Pittsburgh General Text Collection (hosted by University of Pittsburgh's Digital Research Library).
11. Ibid.
12. "Ohio History Central," "John Brickell," ohiohistorycentral.org.
13. "William Brickle" [*sic*], Jefferson County Court House, Steubenville, Ohio, will bk. 3: 416–22.

14. *American Union*, "William Breckle" [*sic*], April 22, 1843, 3.

15. Doyle, *Twentieth Century History of Steubenville*, 391.

16. "William Brickle" [*sic*] will, 416; Steubenville, Ohio 1820 Federal Census, "Wm. Brickler" [*sic*]; 1830 Federal Census, "Wm Brickle" [*sic*]; 1840 Federal Census, "William Brickell."

17. *Miami Metropolis*, "Mr. W.B. Brickell, a Pioneer Citizen, Expired at Ripe Old Age."

18. "Ohio History Central," "Steubenville, Ohio," ohiohistorycentral.org.

19. "Gold Rush Chronology," comspark.com/chronicles.

20. "William Briskell" [*sic*] is listed with a group of men from Steubenville, Ohio, on their way to the gold fields of California in "Movements of California Emigrants on the Western Frontier," *St. Louis Republican*, April 19, 1849. sfgeneology.com/californiabound/cb104.htm.

21. Dundass, *Journal of Samuel Rutherford Dundass*, 1–7.

22. Parkman, *Oregon Trail*, 42.

23. Dundass, *Journal of Samuel Rutherford Dundass*, 8.

24. Ibid., 11.

25. Ibid., 13.

26. Ibid., 54.

CHAPTER 2

27. Perrine, *True Story of Some Eventful Years*, 128.

28. Ibid., 127.

29. Ibid.

30. Rerick, *Memoirs of Florida*, 445.

31. Munroe and Gilpin, *The Commodore's Story*, 69.

32. Ibid., 70.

33. Brickell, "Maude Brickell Manuscript," 1.

34. E-mail exchange between Beth Brickell and Thomas Carey, librarian, San Francisco History Center, San Francisco Public Library, May 26, 27, 2009.

35. E-mail exchange between Beth Brickell and Michael Gillman, librarian, Sacramento Public Library, May 27, 2009.

36. Perrine, *True Story of Some Eventful Years*, 145.

37. Ibid., 142.

38. "Life of a Forty-Niner," kidport.com.

39. *Nov 3, 1851: The Shipping Gazette and Sydney General Trade List*, vol. 9, no. 449 (November 6, 1852).

CHAPTER 3

40. "Arrivals," *The Shipping Gazette and Sydney General Trade List*, vol. 9, no. 449 (November 6, 1852).

41. Monaghan, *Australians and the Gold Rush*, 213–15.

42. McMahon and Wild, *American Fever, Australian Gold*, 206–27.

43. McMahon and Wild, "William Barnwell Brickell in Australia," 5–18.

44. McMahon and Wild, *American Fever, Australian Gold*, 209.

45. McMahon and Wild, "William Barnwell Brickell in Australia," 7.
46. Monaghan, *Australians and the Gold Rush*, 173.
47. Heritageaustralia.com.
48. Monaghan, *Australians and the Gold Rush*, 196.
49. Ibid.
50. Ibid., 225.
51. Ibid., 195.
52. "The Australian Gold Rush," patricktaylor.com/Australian-gold-rush.
53. McMahon and Wild, *American Fever, Australian Gold*, 603.
54. Denise McMahon e-mail to Beth Brickell, April 5, 2009.
55. McMahon and Wild, *American Fever, Australian Gold*, 210.
56. "William Barnwell Brickell," application for naturalization, October 20, 1856, State Archives NSW: NRS 1040, 4/1200, roll: 129, register no. 1, 771.
57. McMahon and Wild, *American Fever, Australian Gold*, 211, 605.
58. "Timeline Albury," Albury City Library Museum website.
59. *Mariners and Ships in Australian Waters*, "The State Records Authority of New South Wales," marners.records.nsw.gov.au.
60. Ibid.
61. Monaghan, *Australians and the Gold Rush*, 229, 230.
62. McMahon and Wild, "William Barnwell Brickell in Australia," 11.
63. McMahon and Wild, *American Fever, Australian Gold*, 212.
64. Ibid.
65. McMahon and Wild, "William Barnwell Brickell in Australia," 10.
66. Monaghan, *Australians and the Gold Rush*, 228.

CHAPTER 4

67. McMahon and Wild, "William Barnwell Brickell in Australia," 9.
68. *New South Wales Government Gazette*, issue 19, 242 (February 18, 1848), and issue 41 (April 8, 1851).
69. Denise McMahon e-mail exchange with Beth Brickell, June 16, 2009, in which McMahon cites a report of the sale of land to Bulmer at an auction.
70. "Amy Alice Bulmer," New South Wales birth certificate, registration number 6653/1857, February 3, 1857. Retrieved from New South Wales Registry of Births, Deaths and Marriages.
71. William Brickell–Mary Bulmer marriage certificate of May 20, 1862, "Marriages Solemnized in District of Bourke," sch. C, 1962, no. 244. Retrieved from New South Wales Registry of Births, Deaths and Marriages.
72. Maude Brickell, "Maude Brickell Manuscript," 1.
73. Woodlawn Cemetery, Miami, Emma Stanhope Brickell; Bonawit, *Miami, Florida, Early Families*, 69.
74. Bonawit, *Miami, Florida, Early Families*, 69.
75. Denise McMahon e-mail exchange with Beth Brickell, April 1, 2009.
76. *Miami Metropolis*, "Mr. W.B. Brickell, a Pioneer Citizen, Expired at Ripe Old Age."
77. Joseph Bulmer death certificate of May 23, 1858, New South Wales, registration no. 1858/002433. Retrieved from New South Wales Registry of Births, Deaths and Marriages.

78. McMahon and Wild, *American Fever, Australian Gold*, 214.

79. Denise McMahon e-mail to Beth Brickell, May 13, 2009.

80. McMahon and Wild, *American Fever, Australian Gold*, 215–18.

81. Ibid., 607, 611.

82. McMahon and Wild, "William Barnwell Brickell in Australia," 12.

83. Ibid.

84. Ibid.

CHAPTER 5

85. McMahon and Wild, "William Barnwell Brickell in Australia," 12.

86. Maude Brickell, "Maude Brickell Manuscript," 1.

87. *Biographical Review*, "David Z. Brickell," 334–38.

88. *Biographical Review*, "David Z. Brickell," 337; *Directory of Pittsburgh and Allegheny Cities 1864–1865*, "David Z. Brickell."

89. "List of Exempts, Sixth Ward," *The Rebellion Record of Allegheny County from April 1861 to October 1862*, Historic Pittsburgh Collection, 6.

90. *Biographical Review*, 338.

91. Killikelly, *History of Pittsburgh*, 212.

92. Brickell, "Maude Brickell Manuscript," 2.

93. *Biographical Review*, 338.

94. *Miami Metropolis*, "Mr. W.B. Brickell, a Pioneer Citizen, Expired at Ripe Old Age."

95. Brickell, "Maude Brickell Manuscript," 2.

96. Angel Price, "Whitman's *Drum Taps* and Washington's Civil War Hospitals," xroads.virginia.edu; "Washington D.C. War Hospitals," pa-roots.com.

97. Price, "Whitman's *Drum Taps* and Washington's Civil War Hospitals."

98. Ibid.

99. Ibid.

100. Ibid.

101. Ibid.

102. Brickell, "Maude Brickell Manuscript," 2.

103. Killikelly, *History of Pittsburgh*, 215.

104. Boucher, *History of Westmoreland*, 504, 505; Perick and Howard, *Jeannette*, 38; *Biographical Review*, 338.

105. Killikelly, *History of Pittsburgh*, 213.

106. McMahon and Wild, "William Barnwell Brickell in Australia," 12; information from Public Records Office, Victoria, Australia, "Outward Passengers to Interstate, UK, NZ & Foreign Ports 1852–1870." Retrieved from prov.vic.gov.au.

107. Cleveland city directories for 1869–70, 84; 1870–71, 87; 1871–72, 91; "1886 Sanborn Fire Insurance Maps of Cleveland," plate 9, vol. 1, and plate 41, vol. 2; Cuyahoga County Recorder's Office deeds, bk. 135: 420, and bk. 179: 627.

108. Van Tassel and Grabowski, *Encyclopedia of Cleveland History*, "Henry M. Flagler."

109. Sewell, *Memoirs and History of Miami*, 75, quoting from a biographical sketch of the Brickells in no. 1, vol. 1 of *Miami Metropolis*, May 15, 1896.

110. Bell, "'When I Die,' Said Maude, 'Write Me a Story, Jack.'"

111. *Literary Digest*, "He Made Florida," 1240.

112. "Ohio History Central," "John D. Rockefeller." ohiohistorycentral.org.

113. "The Standard Oil Company," scripophily.net.

114. Kearney, *Mostly Sunny Days*, 25; "Henry Morrison Flagler Biography," retrieved from flaglermuseum.org; Van Tassel and Grabowski, *Encyclopedia of Cleveland History*, "Henry M. Flagler."

115. Brickell, "Maude Brickell Manuscript," 1.

116. Tarbell, *History of the Standard Oil Company*, 43.

117. Ibid., 44.

118. Ibid., 47.

119. Van Tassel and Grabowski, *Encyclopedia of Cleveland History*, "John D. Rockefeller."

120. Chernow, *Titan*, 146–47.

121. Tarbell, *History of the Standard Oil Company*, 50.

122. Ibid.

123. Chernow, *Titan*, 142–43.

124. Ibid.

125. "Ohio History Central," "John D. Rockefeller." ohiohistorycentral.org.

126. Bonawit, *Miami, Florida, Early Families*, 69.

127. Ash, "The Settler Who Sailed in on His Yacht."

128. "Henry Beilstein vs. William B. Brickell," *Annals of Cleveland Court Record Series, 1867–1868*, June 6, 1867, February Term, 1868, CP 17–33:358, Abstract 30: 35.

129. *Miami Herald*, "Brickell Mansion Was Built in 1871."

130. Wm. B. Brickell handwritten letter to W.H. Branch, January 30, 1867, "Branch Family Collection," University of North Carolina, Chapel Hill's Wilson Library Special Collections.

131. Peters, *Biscayne Country*, 8, quoting from a September 30, 1875 letter written by Frances (Mrs. Ephraim) Sturtevant that was printed in the *Cleveland Herald* and later reprinted in the *Semi-Tropical*.

132. Ibid.

133. Townshend, *Wild Life in Florida*, 8.

134. *Miami Herald*, "Brickell Mansion Was Built in 1871."

135. Harriet English to William Brickell, Power of Attorney of June 24, 1870, recorded December 10, 1889, Miami-Dade County Recorder's Office/Records Library, Misc. Records bk. A, 138, 139.

136. *Mrs. Hagan (or Rebecca Egan) Donation Abstract of Title*, 3.

137. Ibid., 4.

138. Although the family name was Egan, when the land grant was recorded the name was misspelled to conform with the way the name was pronounced at Key West at the time. A later legal proceeding corrected the mistake, and the "Hagan" name was changed to Egan after a family with the actual name of Hagan filed a lawsuit against the Brickells claiming ownership to the land.

139. Harriet English to Mary Brickell Deed of February 25, 1874, recorded February 14, 1883, Miami-Dade County Recorder's Office/Records Library, deed. bk. 253, 19. The deed notes a total conveyance of 2,550 acres, but later surveys reduced the total to 2,507.83 acres.

140. Robinson, *Tropical Frontier*, 546.

Chapter 6

141. Helen Muir, "Voices from the Past," Becky Roper Matkov, ed., *Miami's Historic Neighborhoods: A History of Community* (Miami, FL: Historical Publishing Network, 2001), 15.

142. George Parsons, diary entry of April 3, 1874, "Diaries 1872–1875 by George Whitwell Parsons," University of Florida, Gainesville.

143. Woodlawn Cemetery, Miami, personal visit and records retrieved February 15, 2009.

144. Parsons diary entry of April 3, 1874.

145. U.S. Federal Census, Dade County, Florida, June 1880.

146. Woodlawn Cemetery, Miami records.

147. Brickell, "Maude Brickell Manuscript," 2.

148. E.T. Sturtevant lien against William B. Brickell in amount of $2,970 for "labor and materials," December 23, 1871, Miami-Dade County Recorder's Office/Records Library, legal bk. 8.

149. Frances (Mrs. E.T.) Sturtevant, letter to *Cleveland Herald* (January 1876). Reprinted in *Semi-Tropical* (March 1876).

150. Townshend, *Wild Life in Florida*, 235.

151. Covington, *Seminoles of Florida*, 1–27.

152. Carr, "The Brickell Store and Seminole Trade," 180.

153. Kersey, "Private Societies and the Maintenance of Seminole Tribal Integrity."

154. Carr, "The Brickell Store and Seminole Trade," 183.

155. Branning, "Apartment Marks Historic Site."

156. Brickell, "Maude Brickell Manuscript," 2; Trumbull, "Two Women Were Miami's Pioneers."

157. Kersey, *Pelts, Plumes and Hides*, 32, quoting from W.B. Brickell letter to commissioner of Indian Affairs of June 15, 1891.

158. *Miami Metropolis*, "Mr. W.B. Brickell, a Pioneer Citizen, Expired at Ripe Old Age"; Gaby, *Miami River*, 42.

159. Kersey, *Pelts, Plumes, and Hides*, 34.

160. Rose Wagner (Mrs. A.C.) Richards, "Reminiscences of the Early Days of Miami," paper #8.

161. Brickell, "Maude Brickell Manuscript," 2; Carr, "The Brickell Store," 183.

162. Brickell, "Maude Brickell Manuscript," 3; Carr, "The Brickell Store," 183.

163. Brickell, "Maude Brickell Manuscript," 2.

164. Peters, *Lemon City*, 28.

165. Oyer, "Legend of the Barefoot Mailman," 20; Kearney, *Mostly Sunny Days*.

166. Perrine, *True Story of Some Eventful Years*, 296.

167. Emma (Mrs. Vincent) Gilpin diary, "Gilpin Family Collection," Historical Museum of Southern Florida, Miami.

168. Perrine, *True Story of Some Eventful Years*, 296.

169. H.G. traveling with Joseph H. Day, "Journal of a Trip of the Miamia, 1877," June 1, 1877 entry. The diary is at the Florida Historical Society Library, Cocoa, Florida, with a copy at the Historical Museum of Southern Florida, Miami.

170. Ibid.

171. Perrine, *True Story of Some Eventful Years*, 296.

172. Ibid.
173. *Encyclopaedia Britannica*, "Emu" (Chicago: William Benton, 1964).
174. Perrine, *True Story of Some Eventful Years*, 296.
175. H.G. "Journal," June 1, 1877 entry.
176. Perrine, *True Story of Some Eventful Years*, 296.
177. Affidavit of Edgar Baker, March 11, 1880, Miami-Dade County Recorder's Office/Records Library, legal bk.: 148.

CHAPTER 7

178. Parks, *Miami, The Magic City*, 42.
179. Wagner, "Early Pioneers of South Florida," 65.
180. Dade County Commission Minutes, 1868–1876.
181. Parks, *Miami, The Magic City*, 42.
182. Peters, *Biscayne Country*, 26.
183. Ibid.
184. Parks, *Miami, The Magic City*, 42.
185. Dade County Commission Minutes, November 4, 1872.
186. Ibid., October 30, 1872.
187. Peters, *Biscayne Country*, 30.
188. Munroe and Gilpin, *The Commodore's Story*, 54.
189. Rose Wagner (Mrs. A.C.) Richards, "Reminiscences of the Early Days of Miami," paper #9.
190. Dade County Commission Minutes, October 30, 1874.
191. Rose Wagner (Mrs. A.C.) Richards, "Reminiscences of the Early Days of Miami," paper #9.
192. Peters, *Biscayne Country*, 30.
193. Rose Wagner (Mrs. A.C.) Richards, "Reminiscences of the Early Days of Miami," paper #11.
194. Robinson, *Tropical Frontier*, 83.
195. Dade County Commission Minutes, 1877–1879.
196. Rose Wagner (Mrs. A.C.) Richards, "Reminiscences of the Early Days of Miami," paper #7.
197. Munroe and Gilpin, *The Commodore's Story*, 69.
198. "Book Notes" regarding Stuart McIver's *One Hundred Years on Biscayne Bay, 1887–1987, Florida Historical Quarterly* 68, no. 3 (January 1990), 393.
199. Wagner, "Early Pioneers of South Florida," 67.
200. Ash, "The Settler Who Sailed in on His Yacht."
201. Brickell, "Maude Brickell Manuscript," 4.
202. Rockwood, *In Biscayne Bay*, 118.
203. Ibid., 120.
204. "Mariners and Ships in Australian Waters," mariners.records.nsw.gov.au, fiche 544: 004, State Records Authority of New South Wales: Shipping Master's Office; "Passengers Arriving 1855–1922," NGS 13278, [X210] reel 502.
205. *Australian Men of Mark*, vol. 1., "Joseph Bulmer, Jr." (Sydney: Charles F. Maxwell, 1889), film 1439042: 36.

CHAPTER 8

206. Munroe and Gilpin, *The Commodore's Story*, 92.
207. A careful search by the author at the Miami-Dade County Recorder's Office/ Records Library in Miami turned up deeds documenting the purchase of 6,427 acres of land by the Brickells between 1874, when the Harriet English tracts were bought, and 1895, when they began giving land to Henry Flagler for the railroad.
208. Muir, *Miami, U.S.A.*, 7; Gaby, *Miami River*, 1.
209. Gaby, *Miami River*, 35.
210. Sewell, *Memoirs and History of Miami*, 52.
211. *Literary Digest*, "He 'Made' Florida," 1241.
212. "Romance of the Rails," January 24, 1957 speech by Carlton J. Corliss, "Tuttle Family Collection," Historical Museum of Southern Florida.
213. Julia Tuttle's letter and proposal of November 14, 1892, is referred to in Flagler's response to her of April 27, 1893.
214. Letter from H.M. Flagler to Julia Tuttle, April 27, 1893, "Tuttle Family Collection," Historical Museum of Southern Florida.
215. Chandler, *Henry Flagler*, 173.
216. Peters, *Miami 1909*, 8.
217. Wiggins, "The Birth of the City of Miami," 8.
218. Kearney, *Mostly Sunny Days*, 26.
219. Chandler, *Henry Flagler*, 169.
220. Robinson, *Tropical Frontier*, quote from Dorn, "Recollections of Early Miami," 560.

CHAPTER 9

221. Ash, "The Settler Who Sailed in on His Yacht."
222. Letter from Thelma Peters to Carter Brickell, October 25, 1991.
223. Letter from Thelma Peters to Carter Brickell, June 12, 1989.
224. Brickell, "Maude Brickell Manuscript," 3.
225. Letter from H.M. Flagler to Julia Tuttle, April 22, 1895. "Tuttle Family Collection," Historical Museum of Southern Florida.
226. Harriet English to Mary Brickell deed of February 25, 1874, recorded February 14, 1883, Miami-Dade County Recorder's Office/Records Library, bk. 253, 19; Florida Land and Mortgage Company to Mary and William B. Brickell deed of January 8, 1890, Miami-Dade County Recorder's Office/Records Library, bk. D: 379–80.
227. Flagler's letter to Tuttle, April 22, 1895, "Tuttle Family Collection," Historical Museum of Southern Florida, Miami.
228. Weidling and Burghard, *Checkered Sunshine*, 18; Dillon and Knetsch, "Forgotten Pioneer," 40; "Stagecoach Visits Fort Lauderdale in 1893," from the *Titusville Advocate*, reprinted in the *Tropical Sun*, March 9, 1893, *Broward Legacy* 9, no. 1, 2: 37.
229. Weidling and Burghard, *Checkered Sunshine*, 19; Dillon and Hobby, "The Riparian Rights Lawsuit," 5.

230. Weidling and Burghard, *Checkered Sunshine*, 19.

231. Wiggins, "The Birth of the City of Miami," 21.

232. Kleinberg, "Signing City's 'Birth Certificate,'" C-4. The article includes a transcription of the Flagler-Tuttle contract.

233. *Miami Metropolis*, "City of Miami," 5, cited by Wiggins in "The Birth of the City of Miami," 32. The *Metropolis* article, retrieved from the historic archive at palmbeachpost.com, mistakenly cites June 12, 1895, as the date of both the Tuttle and Brickell contracts with Flagler, but the Tuttle contract, reproduced in its entirety in Howard Kleinberg's *Miami: The Way We Were*, clearly shows the date of the Tuttle contract was October 24, 1895.

234. Mary and William B. Brickell to Jacksonville, St. Augustine & Indian River Railway Co. of Florida, August 29, 1895, Miami-Dade County Recorder's Office/Records Library, deed bk. J: 83.

235. Julia D. Tuttle to Henry M. Flagler (8 ac.), February 1, 1896, and Julia D. Tuttle to J.E. Ingraham and Henry M. Flagler (92 ac.), February 1, 1896, Miami-Dade County Recorder's Office/Records Library, deed bk. Q: 262, 257.

236. William B. and Mary Brickell to East Coast Railway Co. (100' strip), bk. O: 229, and (one lot), bk. O: 275, April 24, 1896; William B. and Mary Brickell to Fort Dallas Land Co. (multiple lots), bk. O: 257, May 1, 1896. Miami-Dade County Recorder's Office/Records Library deed books.

237. William B. and Mary Brickell to Fort Dallas Land Co. (multiple lots), bk. V: 14, December 27, 1897; Fort Dallas Land Co. to Mary and W.B. Brickell (multiple lots), bk. R: 459, March 24, 1898; Fort Dallas Land Co. to Mary Brickell (3 lots), bk. R: 462, April 30, 1898; William B. and Mary Brickell (one block), bk. R: 17, April 30, 1898. Miami-Dade County Recorder's Office/Records Library deed books.

238. Mary and William B. Brickell to Fort Dallas Land Co. (multiple lots), bk. Q: 341, January 6, 1897; Julia D. Tuttle to Fort Dallas Land Co. (multiple lots), bk. Q: 347, January 6, 1897. Miami-Dade County Recorder's Office/Records Library deed books.

239. Harriet English to Mary Brickell, February 25, 1874, recorded February 13, 1883, Miami-Dade County Recorder's Office/Records Library, deed bk. A: 267.

240. Scott, "The Many Heirs of Jonathan Lewis," 2–23.

241. William B. and Mary Brickell quitclaim deed to Julia Tuttle of 100 ac. tract known as the John Eagan (Egan) Grant, January 15, 1896, Miami-Dade County Recorder's Office/Records Library, deed bk. N: 343.

242. Brickell, "Maude Brickell Manuscript," 3.

243. Harriet English to J.V. Harris, MD (740 ac.), November 30, 1869, Key West–Dade County Recorder's Office, deed bk. G: 475.

Chapter 10

244. Letter from H.M. Flagler to Julia Tuttle, July 20, 1896, Historical Museum of Southern Florida, "Tuttle Family Collection."

245. Letter from H.M. Flagler to Julia Tuttle, August 10, 1896, HMSF.

246. Letter from H.M. Flagler to Julia Tuttle, August 24, 1896, HMSF.

247. Letter from H.M. Flagler to Julia Tuttle, December 8, 1896, HMSF.

248. Letter from J.E. Ingraham to Julia Tuttle, October 26, 1897, HMSF.
249. Letter from W.S. Graham to J.R. Parrott, February 24, 1896.
250. Ibid.
251. *Miami Metropolis*, "City of Miami," 5.
252. Dade County Commission Minutes, December 10, 1895, 342; April 22, 1996, 366.
253. Peters, ed., *Memoirs of Estelle DesRochers Zumwalt*.
254. Cohen, *Historical Sketches*, 11.
255. Kersey, *Pelts, Plumes and Hides*, 36.
256. Munroe and Gilpin, *The Commodore's Story*, 255.
257. Whited, "Glittering Hotel Can't Dim Glow of Bygone Days."
258. *Miami Metropolis*, "Wm. B. Brickell, Sr."
259. Letter from Emma (Mrs. Vincent) Gilpin, April 6, 1899, Historical Museum of Southern Florida, "Gilpin Collection."
260. Brickell, "Maude Brickell Manuscript," 3.
261. "Unassisted Immigrant Passenger Lists, 1826–1922," New South Wales, Australia.
262. Rerick, *Memoirs of Florida*, 17.
263. "Unassisted Immigrant Passenger Lists, 1826–1922," NSW.
264. Munroe and Gilpin, *The Commodore's Story*, 255.
265. Ibid.
266. Letter from Thelma Peters to Carter Brickell, September 27, 1985.

CHAPTER 11

267. Brickell, "An Announcement to the People of Miami."
268. Kleinberg, "Signing City's 'Birth Certificate,'" 4C.
269. Ibid.
270. Sewell, *Memoirs and History of Miami*, 93, quoting from the *Miami Metropolis*, no. 1, vol. 1, May 15, 1896.
271. Knetsch, "Not Everyone Liked the Brickells," 13.
272. Brickell, "An Announcement to the People of Miami."
273. Mary Brickell to City of Miami, Miami-Dade County Recorder's Office/Records Library, deed bk. 102: 368.
274. Ash, "The Settler Who Sailed in on His Yacht."
275. Brickell, "An Announcement to the People of Miami."
276. Ibid.
277. Mary Brickell to James Deering, January 5, 1914, Miami-Dade County Recorder's Office/Records Library, deed bk. 120: 20.
278. Straight, "Early Miami through the Eyes of Youth," 71.
279. Wood, "Mary Bulmer Brickell."
280. George Parsons, "Diaries 1872–1875 by George Whitwell Parsons," University of Florida, Gainesville.
281. *Miami Herald*, "Mrs. Mary Brickell Will Be Buried."
282. *Miami Herald*, "Beautiful Brickell Hammock Subdivision."
283. *Miami Herald*, "Brickell Hammock Tract is Sold Out."

284. "Plat of Riverside, Brickell's Addition in City of Miami, Florida," Miami-Dade County Recorder's Office/Records Library, plat bk. 4: 45, October 1913.

285. Riverside expansion by Mary Brickell, Miami-Dade County Recorder's Office/Records Library, plat bk. 5: 43, December 30, 1919.

286. "Colee Hammock, Mrs. Mary Brickell's Subdivision," Miami-Dade County Recorder's Office/Records Library, plat bk. I: 17, March 22, 1920; "Rio Vista," Miami-Dade County Recorder's Office/Records Library, plat bk. I: 18, October 22, 1920.

287. Maude E. Brickell, Frank Clark and William B. Brickell Jr., Executors of the Estate of Mary Brickell, deceased, to C.J. Hector, June 10, 1924, Miami-Dade County Recorder's Office/Records Library, deed bk. 36: 47; "C.J. Hector's Re-Subdivision of Rio Vista," Miami-Dade County Recorder's Office/Records Library, plat bk. I: 24.

288. *Brickell v. Town of Ft. Lauderdale*, 75 Fla. 622, 78 So. 681, Florida Supreme Court, April 26, 1918.

289. Mary Brickell to City of Miami, February 1, 1898, Miami-Dade County Recorder's Office/Records Library, deed bk. S: 335.

290. "Reclaiming the Everglades," "David Grandison Fairchild," everglades.fiu.edu/reclaim/bios/fairchild.htm.

291. Cohen, *Historical Sketches*, 210–11.

292. Mary Brickell to City of Miami, August 9, 1921, Miami-Dade County Recorder's Office/Records Library, deed bk. 323: 298.

293. Muir, "The Puzzling Brickell Legend."

294. Mary Brickell to City of Miami (10 ac. for $750), June 24, 1897, Miami-Dade County Recorder's Office/Records Library, deed bk. M: 188.

295. Judith S. Pruitt, "The Miami Women's Heritage Trail," Dade Heritage Trust, 2000.

296. *Miami Herald*, "Mrs. Mary Brickell Will Be Buried."

297. Muir, *Miami, U.S.A.*, 88.

298. Ibid., 44.

299. *Miami Herald*, "Colored People Mourn Mrs. Brickell's Passing."

300. Wood, "Mary Bulmer Brickell."

301. *Miami Herald*, "Blanton Allows a Large Sum for Handling Estate."

302. Ibid.

303. "Confirms the Title of Brickell Estate to $12,000,000 Land," May 4, 1923. Newspaper article in "Brickell Family Collection," Historical Museum of South Florida.

304. Howard Kleinberg, "Miami's First Newspaper."

305. Munroe and Gilpin, *The Commodore's Story*, 70.

306. Mooney, "Local Deaths: William Brickell, Well-Known Film, TV Stuntman."

Chapter 12

307. Information for this article is from an interview with Carmen Petsoules by the author on May 2, 2009. Facts have been confirmed with numerous newspaper clippings and documents.

308. Carr and Ricisak, "Preliminary Report," 282.

309. Mary Brickell to City of Miami, August 9, 1921, Miami-Dade County Recorder's Office/Records Library, deed bk. 323: 298.
310. "Proclamation City of Miami, Florida," signed by Stephen P. Clark, mayor, December 8, 1995.
311. Letter to Carmen Petsoules from Becky Roper Matkov, executive director, Dade Heritage Trust, May 8, 1998.

Bibliography

Manuscript Collections

Brickell, Maude. Transcription of autobiographical sketch. Historical Museum of Southern Florida, Miami, "Brickell Family Collection."

Brickell, William B. Letter to W.H. Branch, January 30, 1867. Wilson Library Special Collections, University of North Carolina, Chapel Hill, "Branch Family Collection."

Deering, James. Letter to Mary Brickell, February 15, 1915. Historical Museum of Southern Florida, Miami, "Brickell Family Collection."

Gilpin, Emma. Letters. Historical Museum of Southern Florida, Miami, "Gilpin Family Collection."

Gleason, William. Papers, 1869–1949. P.K. Yonge Library of Florida History, University of Florida, Gainesville, "Gleason Family Papers."

H.G. Journal, 1877. Florida Historical Society Library, Cocoa, Florida. Copy at Historical Museum of Southern Florida, Miami.

Historical Museum of Southern Florida, Miami. Brickell Family Collection.

———. Brickell Personal Correspondence.

———. Diary of unknown Cocoanut Grove girl, 1908.

———. Douglass, Andrew Ellicott, diary and letters, 1881–1885.

———. Florida East Coast Railway file.

———. Gilpin Collection.

———. Peters (Thelma) Collection.

———. Tuttle Family Collection.

Model Land Company Records. Otto G. Richter Library, University of Miami. Collection 75.

Parsons, George Whitwell. Manuscript diary, 1872–1875. P.K. Yonge Library of Florida History, University of Florida, Gainesville.

Peters, Dr. Thelma, letters to Carter Brickell. Beth Brickell private collection.

Petsoules, Carmen, private collection. Matkov, Becky Roper, Dade Heritage Trust, letter to Carmen Petsoules, May 8, 1998.
———. "Proclamation City of Miami, Florida," Stephen P. Clark, Mayor, December 8, 1995.

Books

Akin, Edward N. *Flagler: Rockefeller Partner and Florida Baron*. Kent, OH: Kent State University Press, 1988.

Ammidown, Margot. *The Wagner Family: Homesteading in Miami's Pioneer Era, 1855–1896*. N.p.: 1981.

Anderson, Marie. *Julia's Daughters: Women in Dade's History*. Miami: Herstory of Florida, 1980.

Blackman, E.V. *Miami and Dade County, Florida: Its Settlement, Progress and Achievement*. Chuluota, FL: Mickler House, 1977.

Chandler, David Leon. *Henry Flagler: The Astonishing Life and Times of the Visionary Robber Baron Who Founded Florida*. New York: Macmillan Publishing Co., 1986.

Chernow, Ron. *Titan: The Life of John D. Rockefeller, Sr.* New York: Random House, 1998.

Clark, Thomas D., ed. *Gold Rush Diary: Being the Journal of Elisha Douglass Perkins on the Overland Trail in the Spring and Summer of 1849*. Lexington: University of Kentucky Press, 1967.

Cohen, Isidor Cohen. *Historical Sketches and Sidelights of Miami, Florida*. Miami, FL: privately printed, 1925.

Covington, James W. *The Seminoles of Florida*. Gainesville: University Press of Florida, 1993.

Dundass, Samuel Rutherford. *Journal of Samuel Rutherford Dundass as a Member of the Steubenville Company Bound for San Francisco in the Year 1849*. Steubenville, OH: Conn's Job Office, 1857.

Franken, Harry B. *Columbus, the Discovery City: A Contemporary Portrait*. Chatsworth, CA: Windsor Publications, 1991.

Gaby, Donald C. *The Miami River and Its Tributaries*. Miami: Historical Association of Southern Florida, 1993.

Gannon, Michael V. *Florida: A Short History*. Gainesville: University Press of Florida, 1993.

Hanna, Alfred Jackson, and Kathryn Abbey Hanna. *Florida's Golden Sands*. New York: Bobbs-Merrill Co., 1950.

Henshall, James A. *Camping and Cruising in Florida*. Cincinnati, OH: Robert Clarke & Co., 1884.

Hollingsworth, Tracy. *History of Dade County, Florida*. Coral Gables, FL: Glade House, 1949.

Kearney, Bob, ed. *Mostly Sunny Days: A Miami Herald Salute to South Florida's Heritage*. Miami, FL: Miami Herald Publishing Co., 1986.

Kersey, Harry A., Jr. *Pelts, Plumes and Hides: White Traders Among the Seminole Indians, 1870–1930*. Gainesville: University Press of Florida, 1975.

Killikelly, Sarah Hutchins. *The History of Pittsburgh*. Pittsburgh, PA: Montgomery, 1906.

Kleinberg, Howard. *Miami: The Way We Were*. N.p.: Seaside Publishing Co., 1990.

Knepper, George W. *Ohio and Its People*. Kent, OH: Kent State University Press, 2003.

Knetsch, Joe. *Florida's Seminole Wars, 1817–1858*. Charleston, SC: Arcadia Publishing Co., 2003.

Liles, Harriet Stiger, Ann Spach, Frances G. Hunter and Ann Josberger McFadden Chesney. *Miami Diary 1896: A Day by Day Account of Events That Occurred the Year Miami Became a City*. N.p.: 1996.

Martin, Sidney Walter. *Florida's Flagler*. Athens: University of Georgia Press, 1949.

———. *Henry Flagler: Visionary of the Gilded Age*. Lake Buena Vista, FL: Tailored Tours Publications, 1998.

Martin, William T. *History of Franklin County (Ohio): A Collection of Reminiscences of the Early Settlement of the County with Biographical Sketches and a Complete History of the County to the Present Time*. "John Brickell—His Captivity." Columbus, OH: Follett, Foster & Co., 1858.

McMahon, H. Denise, and Christine G. Wild. *American Fever, Australian Gold: American & Canadian Involvement in Australia's Gold Rush*. Middle Park, Queensland, Australia: 2008.

Monaghan, Jay. *Australians and the Gold Rush: California and Down Under 1849–1854*. Berkeley and Los Angeles: University of California Press, 1966.

Muir, Helen. *Miami, U.S.A.: Expanded Edition*. Gainesville: University Press of Florida, 2000.

Munroe, Ralph M., and Vincent Gilpin. *The Commodore's Story*. New York: Ives Washburn, 1930.

Parkman, Francis, Jr. *The Oregon Trail*. New York: Penguin Classics, 1982.

Parks, Arva Moore. *The Forgotten Frontier: Florida through the Lens of Ralph Middleton Munroe*. Miami, FL: Alina Press, 1977.

———. *Miami the Magic City*. Tulsa, OK: Continental Heritage Press, 1981.

———. *Miami Then & Now*. Miami, FL: Centennial Press, 1992.

Parks, Arva Moore, and Carolyn Klepser. *Miami Then & Now*. San Diego, CA: Thunder Bay Press, 2002.

Parks, Arva Moore, and Gregory W. Bush. *Miami: The American Crossroad*. Needham Heights, MA: Simon & Schuster, 1996.

Perick, Terry, and John Howard. *Images of America: Jeannette, Pennsylvania*. N.p.: n.d.

Perrine, Henry E. *A True Story of Some Eventful Years in Grandpa's Life*. Buffalo, NY: E.H. Hutchinson, 1885.

Peters, Thelma. *Biscayne Country 1870–1926*. Miami, FL: Banyan Books Inc., 1981.

———. *Lemon City: Pioneering on Biscayne Bay 1850–1925*. Miami, FL: Banyan Books Inc., 1976.

———. ed. *Memoirs of Estelle DesRochers Zumwalt, A Miami Pioneer*. Miami, FL: Falco Printing, 1973.

———. *Miami 1909*. Miami, FL: Banyan Books, 1984.

Pierce, Charles W. *Pioneer Life in Southeast Florida*. Donald W. Curl, ed. Coral Gables, FL: University of Miami Press, 1970.

Pruitt, Judith S. *The Miami Women's Heritage Trail*. Miami, FL: Dade Heritage Trust, 2000.

Raibolt, Victor. *The Town That Climate Built* (booklet). N.p.: 1915.

Robinson, Tim. *A Tropical Frontier: Pioneers and Settlers of Southeast Florida, 1800–1890.* Port Salerno, FL: Port Sun Publishing, 2005.

Rockwood, Caroline Washburn. *In Biscayne Bay.* New York: Dodd, Mead and Co., 1891.

Rose, William Ganson. *Cleveland: The Making of a City.* Cleveland, OH: World Publishing Co., 1950.

Sewell, John. *Memoirs and History of Miami, Florida.* Vol. 1. Miami, FL: Franklin Press, 1938.

Sipe, C. Hale. *Fort Ligonier and Its Times: A History of the First English Fort West of the Allegheny Mountains.* Harrisburg, PA: Telegraph Press, 1932.

The Story of a Pioneer (booklet). N.p.: Florida East Coast Railway, n.d.

Studer, Jacob Henry, *Columbus, Ohio: Its History, Resources, and Progress.* N.p.: 1873.

Tarbell, Ida M. *The History of the Standard Oil Company.* Vols. 1, 2. New York: McClure, Phillips & Co., 1904.

Townshend, F. French. *Wild Life in Florida with a Visit to Cuba.* London: Hurst & Blackett, 1875.

Weidling, Philip, and August Burghard. *Checkered Sunshine: The Story of Fort Lauderdale 1793–1955.* Fort Lauderdale, FL: Wake-Brook House, 1974.

REFERENCE SOURCES

Atlas of Cuyahoga County Ohio from Actual Surveys by and Under the Directions of D.J. Lake. Philadelphia: Titus, Simmons & Titus, 1874.

Australian Men of Mark. Vol. 1. "Joseph Bulmer," "Joseph Bulmer, Jr." Sydney, Australia: Charles F. Maxwell, 1889.

Biographical Review: Containing Life Sketches of Leading Citizens of Pittsburgh and the Vicinity, Pennsylvania. Vol. 24. "David Z. Brickell," "William B. Brickell" (brother of D.Z.), "Rev. James Allison" (brother-in-law of D.Z. and W.B.). Boston: Biographical Review Publishing Co., 1897.

Bonawit, Oby J. *Miami, Florida, Early Families & Records.* "The Brickells of Brickell Point–Brickell Avenue." Miami, FL: 1980.

Boucher, John Newton. Edited by John Woolf Jordan. *History of Westmoreland County, Pennsylvania.* Vol. 2. N.p.: Lewis Publishing Co., 1906.

Business Directory, Guide, and History of Dade County: 1896–97. Palm Beach, FL: 1896.

Cable, Kenneth J., and Jane C. Marchant, eds. *Australian Biographical and Genealogical Record, Series 2, 1842–1899.* Vol. 2, grid. ref. B13. Sydney, Australia: Society of Australian Genealogists, 1987.

Cleveland City directories. *Cleveland Directory, 1871–72.* Cleveland, OH: W.S. Robison & Co., 1871.

————. *Cleveland Leader Annual City Directory, 1869–70.* "Euclid Presbyterian Church," "William B. Brickell," "Henry M. Flagler" and "John D. Rockefeller." Cleveland, OH: Leader Book & Job Office, 1869.

————. *Directory of the City of Cleveland, 1870–71.* Cleveland, OH: Wiggins & Weaver, 1870.

Cushing, Thomas. *History of Allegheny County, Pennsylvania.* Chicago: A. Warner Co., 1889.

BIBLIOGRAPHY

Dade County Early Voter Lists, 1836–1920.

Directory of Pittsburgh and Allegheny Cities 1864/1865.

Doyle, Joseph Beatty. *Twentieth Century History of Steubenville and Jefferson County, Ohio and Representative Citizens.* Chicago: Richmond-Arnold, 1910.

Lake, D.J. *Atlas of Cuyahoga County, Ohio.* Philadelphia: Titus, Simmons & Titus, 1874.

Metropolitan Dade County Office of Community Development. *From Wilderness to Metropolis.* Miami, FL: Metropolitan Dade County, 1982.

Pittsburgh Masonic Directory, 1860. "D.Z. Brickell."

Rebellion Record of Allegheny County from April 1861 to October 1862. "List of Exempts, Sixth Ward: Capt. D.Z. Brickell." Pittsburgh, PA: Lare & Hartzel, 1862.

Rerick, Rowland H. *Memoirs of Florida.* Vol. 2. "William Barnwell Brickell." Atlanta, GA: Southern Historical Association, 1902.

Sanborn Fire Insurance Maps of Cleveland. Vols. 1, 2. New York: 1886.

Shipping Gazette and Sydney General Trade List, 1844–1860. Sydney, Australia: John and Charles Fairfax, 1844–1860.

Smith, Percy Frazer. *Notable Men of Pittsburgh and Vicinity.* Pittsburgh, PA: Pittsburgh Printing Co., 1901.

Van Tassel, David D., and John J Grabowski, eds. *The Encyclopedia of Cleveland History.* "Henry M. Flagler" and "John D. Rockefeller." Bloomington: Indiana University, 1987.

ARTICLES

Adams, Eli. "Brickell's All Business; Where the Great Estates and Ornate Mansions Flourished, Rows of Office Buildings Now Make Brickell the Park Avenue of Miami." *Miami Herald*, September 9, 1973, K-1.

Akin, Edward N. "The Cleveland Connection: Revelations from John D. Rockefeller–Julia D. Tuttle Correspondence." *Tequesta* 42 (1982).

Ash, Agnes. "The Settler Who Sailed in on His Yacht." *Miami News*, February 6, 1966.

Balido, Yolanda. "Brickell Bricks Campaign Honors 'Miami's Mother.'" *Miami Herald*, May 15, 1997.

———. "Fondly Remember the Mother of Miami." *Miami Herald*, March 29, 1998.

Becerra, Cesar A. "Mary Brickell Deserves a Bigger Place in History." *Miami Herald*, May 22, 1999.

Bell, Jack. "'When I Die,' Said Maude, 'Write Me a Story, Jack.'" *Miami Herald*, November 24, 1960.

Berning, C.G. "Brickell Point: Trade Post to Tourist Inn." *Miami Herald*, August 22, 1948.

Branning, Don. "Apartment Marks Historic Site." *Miami News*, June 14, 1950.

Brickell, Mary. "An Announcement to the People of Miami Concerning Brickell Hammock." *Miami Herald*, December 10, 1921.

Broward Legacy (Winter/Spring 1994).

———. "Barefoot Path: Florida to Miami" (Winter/Spring 1986): 19.

———. "Stagecoach Visits Fort Lauderdale in 1893" (Winter/Spring 1986).

———. "Stranahan 1893" (Winter/Spring 1986).

Buck, James. "Biscayne Sketches at the Far South." *Tequesta* 9 (1949).

Carballo, Arles. "Project Restoring the Roads." *Miami Herald*, December 2, 1999.

Carr, Robert S. "The Brickell Store and Seminole Indian Trade." *Florida Anthropologist* 36, no. 4 (December 1981).

Carr, Robert S., and John Ricisak. "Preliminary Report on Salvage Archaeological Investigations of the Brickell Point Site, Including the Miami Circle." *Florida Anthropologist* 53, no. 4 (December 2000).

Carr, Robert S., and Ryan J. Wheeler. "The Miami Circle: Fieldwork, Research and Analysis." *Florida Anthropologist* 57, nos. 1–2 (March–June 2004).

Cavanaugh, Joanne. "A Slight Made Right: 'Mother of Miami' Set for New Bridge." *Miami Herald*, January 9, 1994.

Crim, Sara M. "The Story of Lauderdale."

Dillon, Rodney E., Jr., and Daniel T. Hobby. "The Riparian Rights Lawsuit." *New River News* (Summer/Fall 1986).

Dillon, Rodney E., Jr., and Joe Knetsch. "Forgotten Pioneer: The Legacy of Captain William C. Valentine." *Broward Legacy* (Winter/Spring 1994).

Dixon, Eleanor. "Julia Tuttle Rates Title as Our Founder." *Miami Herald*, March 4, 1959.

Dorn, J.K. "Recollections of Early Miami." *Tequesta* 9 (1949).

Faus, Joseph. "Old-Time Residents Recall the Days When Main Industry Was Coontie Root." *Miami News*, September 19, 1948.

Fernandez, Lourdes. "William Brickell; Family Owned the Bayfront." *Miami Herald*, June 1, 1990.

Fichtner, Margaria. "Thelma Peters: Thumbing Through Life's Chapters and Never Looking Back." *Miami Herald*, February 2, 1986.

Florida Historical Quarterly 68, no. 3.

Fryman, Mildred L. "Career of a Carpetbagger: Malachi Martin in Florida." *Florida Historical Quarterly* 56, no. 3.

Gemoules, Craig. "Brickell Family Fights Park Sale." *Miami Herald*, February 5, 1988.

———. "No Bids for Embattled Brickell Park." *Miami Herald*, February 11, 1988.

———. "Park Fight Has Day in Court Today." *Miami Herald*.

George, Paul. "A Cyclone Hits Miami: Carrie Nation's Visit to 'The Wicked City.'" *Florida Historical Quarterly* 58, no. 2.

Graham, W.S. "A Trip to Biscayne Bay." *Titusville Advocate*, February 1893. Reprinted in *The Tropical Sun*, Juno, FL, March 9, 1893.

Kersey, Harry A., Jr. "Private Societies and the Maintenance of Seminole Tribal Integrity, 1899–1957." *Florida Historical Quarterly* 56, no. 3.

Kleinberg, Howard. "The Brickell Mausoleum Sits Vacant." *Miami News* (Jan. 30, 1982).

———. "Growth of a $750-Million Island." *Miami News*.

———. "Miami's First Newspaper and the Centennial That Wasn't." *Miami Herald*, May 15, 1996.

———. "Newfound Pictures of Brickells Enrich Local History." *Miami Herald*, May 19, 1992, A-15.

———. "The 1917 Boom in Apartment Houses." *Miami News*, March 5, 1988.

———. "Signing City's 'Birth Certificate.'" *Miami News*, May 19, 1984, C-4.

———. "South Florida's Modern Breed of Preservationists."

Knetsch, Joe. "Not Everyone Liked the Brickells." *South Florida History*, Historical Association of Southern Florida (Spring 2000).

Kofoed, Jack. "Maude Brickell: Why the Change?" *Miami Herald*, November 24, 1960.

Landers, Helen. "Broward County's Women Pathfinders." *Broward Legacy* (Summer/ Fall 1999).

Literary Digest. "He Made Florida" 46, May 31, 1913.

Martin, Lydia. "Brickell Home Recalls Glory of Old Miami." *Miami Herald*, November 4, 1990.

McLemore, Morris. "The Brickell Place Goes…An Era Ends." *Miami News*, February 14, 1961.

McMahon, Denise, and Christine Wild. "William Barnwell Brickell in Australia." *Tequesta* 67 (2007).

Miami Evening Record. "House Occupied by William Brickell."

Miami Herald. "Beautiful Brickell Hammock Subdivision to Be Monument to Mrs. Brickell Is Plan." December 6, 1921.

———. "Big Building Program in Brickell Hammock." March 10, 1923.

———. "Blanton Allows a Large Sum for Handling Estate." January 24, 1923.

———. "Brickell Estate 60 Years Old." May 10, 1931.

———. "Brickell Estate Willed to Friend." December 19, 1960.

———. "Brickell Hammock Tract Is Sold Out by Day at Auction." February 6, 1923.

———. "Brickell Mansion Was Built in 1871." December 5, 1937.

———. "Brickell Park Swap Back on Agenda for City of Miami." June 14, 1990.

———. "Carol M. Snyder obituary." October 6, 2005.

———. "Colored People Mourn Mrs. Brickell's Passing." January 14, 1922.

———. "Confirms Title of Brickell Estate to $12,000,000 Land." May 4, 1923.

———. "Dade History Recalled." May 23, 1926.

———. "Day to Hold Auction of Gresham Realty in Brickell Hammock." January 23, 1923.

———. "First White Girl Born Here Dies." November 23, 1960.

———. "The Good Old Days." February 22, 1939.

———. "Hundreds of Visitors Arrive in Miami on Board Night Trains." January 28, 1922.

———. "Julia Tuttle More Than a Causeway." May 11, 1999.

———. "Miami Progress Due to Flagler's Vision." December 5, 1937, G-6.

———. "Miami's First Baby and City's Oldest House." October 10, 1954.

———. "Mrs. Mary Brickell Died Suddenly at 12:40 This Morning." January 13, 1922.

———. "Mrs. Mary Brickell Will Be Buried on Estate Overlooking Biscayne Bay." January 14, 1922.

———. "Mrs. Tuttle Saw Future for Miami." July 18, 1945.

———. "United Realty Firm Becomes the Owner of Brickell Hammock." February 10, 1923.

———. "When His Father Took Census Here He Counted 97." November 12, 1970.

Miami Metropolis. "Banks of Miami Take Wise Step to Protect Their Depositors." November 18, 1907.

————. "Biographical Sketch of the Brickells." May 15, 1896.

————. "City of Miami, Some Points about the History of the Place." October 9, 1896, 5.

————. "Miami's Apartment Houses Are Among Finest." November 27, 1917.

————. "Mrs. Brickell Lays Claim to Ownership of River Island." July 1, 1916.

————. "Mr. W.B. Brickell, a Pioneer Citizen, Expired at Ripe Old Age." January 14, 1908.

————. "The Punch Bowl Case." March 4, 1898.

————. "Sale of Island in River Mouth by State Trustees May Prevent Improvement of River Channel." July 27, 1916.

————. "Wm. B. Brickell, Sr." July 23, 1897.

Miami Morning News Record. "William B. Brickell Died at Advanced Age." January 15, 1908.

Miami News. "Brickell Will Filed for Probate." April 21, 1961.

————. "Lemon City." September 19, 1948.

————. "Miss Maude of Brickell Fame." November 23, 1960.

————. "The Puzzling Brickell Legend." November 25, 1960.

Mooney, Jennifer. "Local Deaths: William Brickell, Well-Known Film, TV Stuntman." *Miami Herald*, October 16, 2003.

Muir, Helen. "The Puzzling Brickell Legend." *Miami News*, November 25, 1960, A-15.

New York Herald. "Movements of California Emigrants on the Western Frontier." "Steubenville, Ohio Company: William Briskell [*sic*]." May 10, 1849.

Oyer, Harvey. "Legend of the Barefoot Mailman." *South Florida History* 28, no. 4 (Fall/Winter 2000).

Parks, Arva Moore. "History Is Where You Find It." In *Miami's Historic Neighborhoods: A History of Community*, edited by Becky Roper Markov. San Antonio, TX: Historical Publishing Network, 2001.

————. "Miami in 1876." *Tequesta* 35 (1975).

————. "A Woman's Place." March 2000.

Richards, Adam C. "Dade County in Its Earlier Days." *Miami Herald*, March 3, 1918.

————. "Dade History Recalled." *Miami Herald*, May 23, 1926.

Richards, Rose Wagner. "Reminiscences of the Early Days of Miami." *Miami News*, 1903. Scrapbook no. 3, papers no. 5–11. Agnew Welsh Collection. Miami-Dade Public Library, Florida Room.

Scott, Patrick. "The Many Heirs of Jonathan Lewis." *Broward Legacy* 17, nos. 3–4 (Summer/Fall 1994).

Smiley, David. "One 'Last Hurrah.'" *Miami Herald*, December 31, 2006.

Stout, Wesley. "Beachcomber: Road to Bay Biscayne Ferry." *The Tropical Sun*, December 7, 1967.

Straight, William M. "Early Miami Through the Eyes of Youth." *Tequesta* 53 (2003).

Tanfani, Joseph. "History Buff Finds Rare Brickell Photo." *Miami Herald*, May 7, 1992.

Tomb, Geoffrey. "Read All About It: Miami's 1st Newspaper." *Miami Herald*, May 12, 1996.

————. "Victory for 'The Mary Brickell Lady.'" *Miami Herald*, March 31, 1998.

Trumbull, Steve. "Two Women Were Miami's Pioneers." *Miami Herald*, April 26, 1960, 2.

Wagner, Henry J. "Early Pioneers of South Florida." *Tequesta* 9 (1949).

Waters, Exie. "High Adventure and Epic Romance Have Been Seen and Experienced by Mr. & Mrs. A.C. Richards." *Miami Herald*, 1926. "Miami Book, no. 38," Agnew Welsh Collection. Miami-Dade Public Library, Florida Room.

Whited, Charles. "Glittering Hotel Can't Dim Glow of Bygone Days." *Miami Herald*, 1980.

Wiggins, Larry. "The Birth of the City of Miami." *Tequesta* 55 (1995).

Wilson, F. Page. "Miami: From Frontier to Metropolis: An Appraisal." *Tequesta* 14 (1954).

Wood, Jane. "Julia Tuttle Dreamed of Building a City." *Miami News*, March 4, 1958.

———. "Mary Bulmer Brickell a Mother of Miami." *Miami News*, March 3, 1958.

Zoretich, Frank. "Image of Pioneer Mary Brickell Will Be Added to Brickell Bridge." *Miami Herald*, December 16, 1993.

NEWSPAPERS AND JOURNALS

American Union (Steubenville, OH)
Broward Legacy: A Journal of South Florida History (Fort Lauderdale, FL)
Florida Anthropologist (Pensacola, FL)
Florida Historical Quarterly, Florida Historical Society (Cocoa, FL)
Literary Digest (New York)
Miami Evening Record
Miami Herald
Miami Metropolis
Miami Morning News Record
Miami News
New River News (Fort Lauderdale, FL)
New York Herald
Semi-Tropical (Jacksonville, FL)
South Florida History, Historical Association of Southern Florida (Miami, FL)
Tequesta, Journal of the Historical Association of Southern Florida (Miami, FL)
Titusville Advocate (Titusville, FL)
The Tropical Sun (Juno, FL)

GOVERNMENT RECORDS

Australia, Commonwealth of. Public Records Office, Passenger Records.

———. Vital Records.

Broward County, Florida. Abstract of Title, Frankie Lewis Donation, 1979.

———. Deed Books.

Cleveland, Ohio. Auditor's Duplicate of Taxes Assessed, 1866, 1869.

———. Court Records, 1867–68.

Cuyahoga County, Ohio (Cleveland). Deed Books.

Dade County, Florida. Abstract of Title, Mrs. Hagan (or Rebecca Egan) Donation, 1907.

———. Commission Minutes, 1870–1893 (Miami-Dade Public Library).

————. Deed Books.

————. Legal Books.

————. Miscellaneous Record Books.

————. Plats.

————. Voter Lists.

Jefferson County, Ohio (Steubenville). Wills and Estates, CP Journals and Will Books.

Key West, Florida. Deed Books.

New South Wales, Australia. Certificates of Naturalization, 1849–1903.

————. Government Gazette, Deeds.

————. State Archives, Group NRS 1040.

————. State Records Authority, Mariners Records.

New York. Immigration and Emigration, New York Passenger Lists, 1820–1957.

Pittsburgh, Pennsylvania. Directory of Pittsburgh and Allegheny Cities, 1864–1865.

San Francisco, California. Mariner Passenger Lists.

Sydney, Australia. Registry of Births, Deaths, and Marriages.

United States of America. Census, 1830, Steubenville, Ohio.

————. Census, 1840, Steubenville, Ohio.

————. Census, 1870, Cleveland, Ohio, Ward 6.

————. Census, 1880, Dade County, Florida.

————. Census, 1880, Pittsburgh, Pennsylvania, Precinct 1, Ward 11.

————. Census, 1900, Miami, Florida, Precinct 4.

Victoria, Australia. Government Gazette.

————. Mariner passenger lists.

————. Registry of Births, Deaths and Marriages, District of Bourke, 1862.

WEBSITES

"Australian Gold Rush." Patricktaylor.com/Australian-gold-rush.

"The Encyclopedia of Cleveland History." "John D. Rockefeller," "Henry M. Flagler." Ech.cwru.edu.

"Gold Rush Chronicles: Gold Rush Chronology 1848–1854." Comspark.com/chronicles.

"Henry Morrison Flagler Biography." Flaglermuseum.us.

"Ohio History Central: An Online Encyclopedia of Ohio History." "John D. Rockefeller," "Henry Flagler." Ohiohistorycentral.org.

"Reclaiming the Everglades: South Florida's Natural History, 1884 to 1934." "David Grandison Fairchild." Everglades.fiu.edu/reclaim/bios/fairchild.htm.

"The Standard Oil Company." Scripophily.net.

"Timeline Albury." Alburyhistory.org.au/timeline.html.

"Washington D.C. War Hospitals." Pa-roots.com.

"Whitman's *Drum Taps* and Washington Civil War Hospitals." Xroads.virginia.edu.

About the Author

Beth Brickell is president of Luminous Films, Inc., and is the writer, producer and director of a trilogy of movies—*A Rainy Day, Summer's End* and *Mr. Christmas*—that has won twenty-five film festival and television awards and been broadcast on PBS, Showtime, A&E and Nickelodeon. Formerly an actress, she starred in the CBS television series *Gentle Ben* and received Emmy consideration for guest starring roles on *Bonanza* and *Hawaii 5-0.* She also has a newspaper background as an investigative reporter and has utilized those talents to research and write *William and Mary Brickell: Founders of Miami and Fort Lauderdale.*

Beth has a BA degree in history and political science from the University of Arkansas in Fayetteville and an MFA degree in film from the American Film Institute in Los Angeles. She lives in Beverly Hills, California.

Visit us at
www.historypress.net